Never Giving Up, Never Giving In

A Family Fighting to the End: A Story of A.L.S.

Pamela M. Woods

PublishAmerica
Baltimore

First printing

PublishAmerica has allowed this work to remain exactly as the author intended, verbatim, without editorial input.

Hardcover 978-1-4560-5071-9
Softcover 978-1-4560-5070-2
PUBLISHED BY PUBLISHAMERICA, LLLP
www.publishamerica.com
Baltimore

Printed in the United States of America

DEDICATION:

In loving memory of my loved ones who have passed away from

A.L.S

Father: Addison L Gutherie 1988
Sister: Suzanne I. Gutherie 2006
Brother: Ronald C. Gutherie 2006
Brother: Richard L. Gutherie 2007
Sister: Linda M. Ward 2011

Some day there will be a cure until then my fight will never end.

Your loved ones may be taken from you,
but no one can take their
MEMORIES.
They will live in your heart
FOREVER

Table of Contents

ACKNOWLEDGEMENTS

I would like to thank my husband Jim for encouraging me to find the words to write when I thought I had no more. My daughter Kimberly, thank you for the pictures you took of grandpa throughout his illness. For you to have had the foresight to keep them in great condition for 22 years was priceless. Joshua, thank you for sharing your inspiring poem with me, I found a meaningful place for it in my book. It will forever be preserved. I want to thank all my friends and family who helped me with my book. As a first time author and not having any guidance I was a fortunate to have their knowledge and expertise.

Amyotrophic Lateral Sclerosis
A.L.S.
Better known as Lou Gehrig's disease

The awareness of ALS was brought to light when the great baseball player Lou Gehrig, who played first base for the New York Yankees back in the 30s, fondly referred to by his fans as the iron horse, came down with a progressive degenerative disease called Amyotrophic Lateral Sclerosis A.L.S, which ended his career. Hence the nick name Lou Gehrig's disease.

A.L.S. is a progressive degenerative disease that causes the nerve cells to weaken and die. It attacks a special kind of nerve cell called a motor neuron—the type of cell that connects the nerve to the muscles allowing the brain to transmit signals that enable us to move.

A simpler explanation if you think of your nerves as a telephone wire connecting to your brain as it travels to your muscles via the spinal cord as they transmitted calls giving them commands to function.

When the nerves shred the telephone wire breaks apart causing your connections to be distorted going to the muscle. Since the brain does not have, any other means to get the message to your muscle in order for them to function you lose all muscle control as they deteriorate and die. Over time the destruction continues—robbing one of their ability to move eventually causing complete paralysis. Unmercifully your mind stays intact giving a person the feeling of a prisoner trapped in his own body. In the end, the lungs collapse leading to their demise. About 5% of patients that come down with A.L.S. end up having Familial A.L.S. the inherited form that my family carries. The only thing that remains the same no matter what type of A.L.S. you have is ***DEATH.***

PROLOGUE

What do you do when life's tragedies strike you down and your world starts to crumble? We all have a tendency to take life for granted as we sit back and watch it happen to others. There is no doubt your heart goes out to those that have been affected how can it not. Nevertheless, life goes on as you take a deep breath and thank God every day it was not you. Then all of a sudden, your life takes a devastated turn as you find yourself facing a **NIGHTMARE!**

This is my story:

My name is Pamela I am the oldest of the eight siblings in the Gutherie family. I would like to take you on our family's journey fighting against an incurable devastated disease called A.L.S. *Amyotrophic Lateral Sclerosis, or* better known as *Lou Gehrig's disease.* As the family tries to do everything humanly possibly to save our Dad fully knowing, the odds were always against us.

As I take you back through the years to the death of our grandma setting the stage to see how this mysterious illness in our family reared its ugly attack supposedly with her. Yet her health document stated cause of death was a heart attack resulting from a stroke, which supposable happened when she had **elective** back surgery that the doctors **recommended** to correct her prior symptom of paralysis in her legs. In the end blamed a ripple effect of many more complications that eventually overcame her body ending her life. Never fully understanding why her death certificate only stated cause of death "heart attack," and never disclosed any other complications she had which was assumed the reason for the stroke.

Yet if it were not for the rumors among the elder relatives in the family of some type of paralyzing leg disorder, you would not be questioning the cause of grandma's death many years later.

What could my Dad do? He could not live his life in fear of the "what-ifs" for the rest of his life. His life had to carry on as he tried to keep those haunting rumors as only shadows in his mind. Until the horrifying day came when it was Dad's turn to fight the biggest battle of his life that's when **our Dad's diagnosis revealed the mysterious illness to be A.L.S. mystery solved!** If that was not enough torment for our family, we discovered ten years after Dad's death this horrendous disease started its assault all over again on his **children!**

CHAPTER 1
Memories of the Heart

Never could I imagine it was possible for me to find the right words to write about our family's experience trying to fight a deadly disease called A.L.S. What I'm about to share with you comes from my heart and what I'm hoping it will do for you is touch your soul as you read it.

It is hard for me to believe it has been 22 years since my Dad passed away. Sitting here struggling to put down my memories of his illness, which has always been traumatic for me to remember, has only become clouded again. For sadly now, just in the last 10 years, I've been facing this devastating disease starting all over again with its attack on us, the siblings.

My memories filled with grief and my heart has not completely healed from his death. At times, it feels like yesterday. I have always thought of myself as this strong-minded, strong willed, type of person. Never did I realize how his illness affected my life until I started to pour my heart out on paper for others to read.

I always was one to keep my emotions inside me, always putting up this image that nothing bothers me. To let anyone know how much I was truly hurting on the inside was definitely beyond me. I figured why bother others with my feelings. Everyone has their own traumatic situations that happen to them during their lifetime, why should I add to their burden and reveal mine. Therefore, my emotions remained in my heart. Constantly thinking about the way my Dad died has kept my heart bleeding for 22 years. Now to be able to share my memories has been so therapeutic for me that I have finally found my release. I can now say my heart has mended.

For me the lesson I have learned from this tragedy is **to appreciate family and life every day before it is too late.** You will soon realize the memories you have shared with your loved ones become your most valuable commodity. For they truly become the fuel to your heart that keeps you going. Your loved ones can be taken from you, but their memories will live on forever!

As I share with you the type of man my Dad was, how he lived his life to the fullest, as he strived to do the best he could in anything he set his mind to. Not only was his family important to him, so was his career.

You will read how he tried to keep the mysterious illness as just a shadow in his mind as he carried on with his life. Yet when he felt unexplainable symptoms happening to his own health, you will see how his journey to seek out information about his family health became his biggest quest. Regrettably, with this terrible disease A.L.S., leading to many trials and tribulations, eventually became the biggest fight of Dad's life.

If I could have one wish, it would be to see a cure for A.L.S. This disease has done enough damage in our family and others around the world. I do not want to see anyone go through what we did trying to save our Dad.

CHAPTER 2
Determination, even in High School—1944

Dad was an achiever even as early as his high school years. It was easy to see what type of man he was determined to be. All his life he set goals for himself, as he worked hard to acquire the knowledge, to give him the determination to achieve them.

I remember once a conversation my brother Rick had with Thom Gutherie, one of Dad's cousins, who grew up with him. He told Rick that he put together a genealogy of the Gutherie family and wanted to share with us some special memorable information he had about Dad in his high school years. Dad never spoke about those years with us. Neither did any of his old high school friends we knew, who remained good friends with Dad throughout most of his married years. Believe me, we would have loved to sit and listen to the stories of their good old days.

Therefore, you can imagine our excitement when Thom sent this genealogy to us. We truly relished what he wrote about Dad. Especially the comment Thom made when he said how much admiration he had for Dad, pointing out to us that Dad became a role model to the rest of the cousins growing up, especially how he excelled in academics, sports and leadership abilities. A side of Dad we never knew, as it was not in his nature to brag. Not only did he have highest academic honors in school, he also earned all City and All State Champion running back for Football in 1944 at Mackenzie High School in Detroit.

Thom also bragged about Dad ranking the highest in the ROTC program ever attained in the Detroit schools up until 1944, going from a Capt. to a Lt. Colonial. I am not sure if that was a great accomplishment since we did not know anything about the program, it just sounded great to us. When I read what Thom said about Dad, there was no doubt in my mind that he was an achiever even early on in his life. Although, I could not help chuckling to myself when he wrote, "you know what your Dad's most significant feat was? He convinced the best-looking cheerleader in the class of 1944, Maxine Spurling my mom, to fall in love with him. In 1946, they were married." Then, he added a quote from the famous commentator Paul Harvey.

"Now you know the rest of the story."

He really summed it up very well for us, even though we received Thom's information about our Dad many years after his death. He truly comforted me at a time in my life when my heart was full of grief. I cannot help holding back the tears of pride when I hear how other people felt about Dad.

CHAPTER 3
Dad's trials and tribulations

In 1955 when he joined Ford Motor Company, his career pretty much started to explode. He became a Senior Product Engineering Designer and held several supervisory and managerial positions. In 1968 assigned to Chief Engineer Special Products Programs Systems and Advance Engineering. In 1974, he transferred to Ford of Europe for three years taking charge of automotive engineering for Ford of Europe. Then in 1977 became Vehicle Design Engineering, Chief Engineer.

In 1985, it was the icing on the cake for his career. That year all his hard work and accomplishments paid off. Dad became Chief Engineer of Ford Motor Company large Car Division and Car Design Development. His claim to fame was the popular Ford Taurus and Sable. In a sense, they were his babies. As a proud father, he took them from the floor of the design room overseeing their development, as they came to life.

He was on his way to be part of the Shakers and Makers within Ford Motor Company, groomed to follow Lewis Veraldi, who was at the time Vice President of Luxury, and Large-Car Engineering and Planning, Car Product Development. All of Dad's hard work was finally paying off. Now it was his time to shine, a time for him to start enjoying all the benefits of his hard work as it took him up the ladder to claim his fame. He truly deserved it. No one could have been prouder of him than his family.

Regrettably, it also was the start of his demise. How sad was it that his journey along the highway of life started changing course, ultimately leading to a dark and fateful dead end. Even though this year started with wonderful memories and amazing accomplishments for him, which I will always treasure, sadly the bad ones will be the ones that will haunt me forever.

CHAPTER 4

Sunday dinners, the beginning of the family nightmares

The day we found out about Dad's devastating news about his illness truly affected my memory forever. It was on a Sunday, our family's normal tradition of having dinner at mom and Dad's house. If by accident, you had made other plans on Sundays, you canceled them fast or you were in big trouble. In fact, the only time any of us missed a Sunday dinner was because one of the kids became sick. Even then, we would flip a coin to see which of the parents would stay home while the other went to dinner.

By this time, five of the siblings were married and started their own families, which definitely made it a full house for dinner. Unfortunately, this particular Sunday was shadowed with Dad confiding in us about his health suspicions. Up until that day, we had no idea there was ever an issue.

In the beginning, the way these Sunday dinners started was very unusual, since Dad was the one that instigated them. It was hard for him to see everyone during the week with his late working hours, so the weekend became family catch up time.

He was very sneaky in the way he handled the so-called inviting everyone to dinner. Since there were so many of us, mom always wanted to take turns cooking for the different families, after all, she was the one doing the cooking. However, that was not good enough for Dad he wanted to see everyone at the same time, he so loved a house filled with family and happy sounds.

We always knew he was the one that was responsible for the inviting, even though he tried very hard not to be so obvious so mom would not yell at him, as he slyly found a round about way to do it. He was such an instigator. Dad always had this comical wit about him, a quality that enhanced his personality, of course, passing that trait on to some of us kids always got us into trouble when we were younger, was that our fault?

You see, his idea was if he planted the suggestion of having the kids over for dinner in Ray's head, my youngest brother, enticing him to make the phone calls to let everyone know mom was cooking dinner and everyone was invited. He fully knew Ray would not get into trouble because he was mom's favorite.

It was easy on our part to come to dinner at a drop of a hat, since we all lived close to mom and Dad as we settled down with our own families. I think the furthest one was only 20 minutes away. No one ever asked us to make that decision it just happened that way.

Cautiously Dad would approach mom to break the news about the kids coming to dinner, of course reversing the blame on us, while using his sly voice saying, "hey mom, guess what, the kids called and asked if they could come to dinner, as he said, "that's a great idea, I'm sure mom won't mind." Mom answering him back yelling, "*WHAT DID YOU SAY!* **THEY'RE NOT ALL COMING, ARE THEY?"**

Deep down inside Dad knew mom really did not mind, it was kind of a back and forth game they played for a while. However, mom never let on to Dad that she was always one step ahead of him and always prepared for us kids anyway. Mom knew, since Dad was working a lot of late hours it was his only time to see all of us. After awhile mom gave into him and he did not have to instigate it anymore. Hence our tradition was born, **"SUNDAY DINNERS."** It was traditions like those we all cherished. To this day, our children talk about the good times they had, to them it always felt like a holiday.

However, looking back at this one particular Sunday still devastates me as I remember. When Dad himself called making sure we were all coming to dinner, made me very suspicious that something was wrong. Telling us he had something to discuss with us and did not want to do it over the phone just reassured me that my suspicions were right. When I hung up the phone, I told Jim something serious is on Dad's mind. Maybe it was only a daughter's intuition but it was a feeling I just could not shake. It soon became apparent when we walked in the door that I was right.

He did not seem to greet us with his usual excitement. In the past, he was always excited to see everyone, just like a little kid pacing back and forth until we all got there. Dad could not wait to get all the grandkids excited, rowdy, and loud. Then when he decided he had enough, he went into the den and watched TV until dinner, leaving the noise in the rest of the house to bug mom. He truly enjoyed all the commotion and noise everyone was making. To him it was always happy noise. On the other hand, the noise was too loud for mom, as they were all in the kitchen bugging her.

It is funny; I can even hear her voice right now yelling at them "kids go outside." Nevertheless, that did not last long, when it became too quiet in the house Dad would call them back in only to get them all excited and rowdy all over again. Like I said, he was a great instigator and certainly loved to tease. I guess after having eight kids it was always hard to have a quiet home, at least for him. Mom being home all the time certainly did not mind the quietness occasionally.

When I walked in the door and made eye contact with Dad the expression on his face made me realize something terrible was on his mind. We all gathered in the kitchen, which was always our favorite spot for the family to hang out, as the younger grandkids were occupied having fun running around the house while the older ones were supposed to be supervising. I could not help noticing this sad expression on Dad's face as he tried hard to hide. I could not shake my intuition. I was scared.

Dad started to choke up struggling to tell us what was on his mind. There was no doubt it was hard for him to get his words out, trying hard to get his composure before he started to talk. All of a sudden, as the kitchen quieted down, he blurted out these words with tears in his eyes, **"I THOUGHT I MADE IT**.*"* We were shocked to hear him say that, it certainly did not make any sense to us as we just stood there with our mouths open looking at each other. The room became so quiet that we did not even hear the kids playing, which was weird because we knew they were.

Our thoughts were in a whirlwind wondering what in the world did he mean by that as we felt totally off guard. We had no idea what was going on. Dad was never one to show his emotions. That is when we knew there was something definitely wrong. Never in our worst nightmare were we prepared to hear what he was about to tell us.

You see, this all started when Dad began to have symptoms of what he thought grandma died from. Realizing he could not hide it from us any more, he knew it was time to tell us about his fears and the potential family health secret that he kept to himself all those years. The only way he knew best was to go back in time and tell us about grandma's situation before she died.

When he started his story, I had a hard time understanding why it was all about grandma's illness; I thought we were talking about his situation. Our voices became loud with confusion asking, "Dad, why in the world are you telling us about grandma now, it was so long ago, we only want to know what's happening to you, what is going on here?"

Dad tried to calm everyone down so he could continue, "just listen to me this is very hard for me to tell you, I need to finish. You see," he said, "when your grandma came to live with us she was having problems walking causing her to use a wheelchair all the time. The doctor told us she needed back surgery to correct her problem in her legs, however, it was unsuccessful. Then she had a stroke, blaming the surgery for it, only complications were there before she had the stroke. Like loss of upper body movement. When she started to have trouble with her breathing, it put too much stress on her heart and it gave out. The doctor said the stroke caused her heart attack, which in turn caused her death, never having any documentation telling us different, there was no other reason to believe anything else.

Yet, hearing rumors that trickled down from the elder relatives of some type of a paralyzing leg disorder was always puzzling to me, but who was I to question the doctors. The older I became the rumors seemed to disappear, there was nothing else happening in the family." I figured if there was something to worry, my parents would have told us long ago, but that never happened, in fact, no one spoke about it. So mom and I assumed there was nothing to worry about and carried on with our lives. Although, now and then I had a hard time shaking that haunting feeling, there were just too many pieces of the puzzle that were missing. It was something I tried hard to suppress for many years, which I thought I did, until now.

At this point, we all just stood there with our mouths open in a state of shock. Never did we hear Dad talk like this before; he was so solemn and sincere it was scaring us. We were trying so hard to try to grasp what he was saying, that the room became so quiet I could actually here the beating of my heart. I was hoping mom was going to interrupt him and say never mind your Dad, this health crisis is only rumors, everything is fine, but she never did.

As we continued to listen to his story he said, "your grandma was only 46 when she died, my instincts told me it wasn't just from a stroke, especially hearing all those rumors." "From time to time, I couldn't help thinking about different types of muscle illness that could have easily caused the same symptoms. Even convincing myself, maybe this illness was related to a certain age." Therefore, when I reached the age of 58, I took a deep breath of relief knowing I was safely past grandma's age of 46 when she became ill. Figuring I was out of the woods so to speak, the mysterious nightmare lifted off my shoulders, I was safe and I did not have to worry anymore. If there was ever a health issue in the family, it no longer pertained to me and I was out of danger."

You could see him struggling as he tried to share his fears of the "what-ifs". When all of a sudden he let out this huge sigh, his eyes became all watery as his voice choked trying to finish his story, still wiping the tears from his eyes, he said, "I think my fears are becoming more of a reality, I may have been wrong all this time."

"I'm starting to notice some changes in my body that I can't explain. It really started to concern me a couple weeks ago when I woke up with this terrible leg cramp in my right leg; it seemed to center in the back of my calf. "At first I believed it was from a strained muscle. It was so bad I woke up mom hoping maybe if she massaged my leg the cramp would go away. For awhile it did. Then it came back with more intensity, and with a lot of pain. This went back and forth for about a month. However, the intensity of the pain never went away.

That is when mom and I decided it was time to tell you kids about this unknown illness." Again with another sigh, "you see I never wanted to let you kids know that maybe somewhere down through the family generations there were some speculation of a serious illness. We figured why did we want it to ruin your life with all that worrying if it was not true. So mom and I made a decision to keep this a secret to ourselves and hoped nothing would ever happen to me." "I now feel this is serious enough to go see a doctor. I need to find out what is causing this problem in my leg. With our family being close it would have been impossible to hide it from you kids any more." The room became very quiet again as we all sat there looking at each other trying to take everything in.

Now, here is a family that even if our Dad went to the doctor for a physical we were concerned. We always had a tendency to blow everything out of proportion. He was never sick so it is no wonder we were in a panic mode now. Trying very hard to pull ourselves together, my sister cried out "what is going on with you Dad, how can this be happening, this is not fair!" Attempting to regain our composure so the grandkids could not hear us became impossible, our voices only got louder and louder with every question. That only caused them to come into the kitchen to see what was going on. We all felt like we were having a bad dream and we could not wake up.

Finally, after all our frustration were out, we started to pull ourselves together, gathering our thoughts and coming to an agreement that we needed to settle down and not panic, at least not yet. We did not want to scare the grandkids. Together we decided the most important thing we could do right now was to keep our composure until Dad saw the doctor. We had to find out for sure what we were dealing with; the only way to do that was to get more answers. Then we could get over this slight hurdle and carry on. Of course never in our worst nightmare did we realize how hard this endeavor was going to be.

Looking around the kitchen to see the looks on everyone's faces I could not help noticing this was the first Sunday dinner at mom's house that we had a lot of left over food, **I cannot imagine why!**

CHAPTER 5
Remembering back in time

That evening the ride home from their house was very quiet. We only lived 20 minutes away but it felt like hours. I found myself drifting from one thought to another. I could not wait to get home so I could go to my room and be by myself. I was trying very hard to keep my composure so my girls would not see me cry. I did not want them to worry about me also. Being teenagers, they were old enough to know that something was not right with grandpa.

The only way mentally I could handle all this worrying and keep my sanity at the same time was to treat Dad's situation as if he was only coming down with a bad virus. **Never giving up** hope that whatever it was, he could recover.

When we arrived home, I went straight up to my room and did not say anything to anyone. My family was very concerned for me but they knew I needed my space. It started to get dark fast but I did not care, I just wanted to be alone. I did not want anyone seeing me cry. I think I cried so much that night my tears just dried up. All I wanted to do was think about something else. Trying hard to pretend this was not really happening, I just sat there in the dark in a complete daze. So much was going through my thoughts that I felt like I was in a whirlwind.

As I went to sleep, my mind started to wander. I found myself seeing my grandma so clearly it was as if I could reach out and touch her. There I was, this 6 year old little girl standing there looking down at my grandma with this sad look on my face. That I knew was when she died. There was never any doubt I remember she died, but the way it happened must have been so traumatic for me, I must have blocked it out of my memory completely. That was the only way I could justify what happen to me that night. Frankly, in a little child's eyes, I can see why those memories of that morning never came back; it was emotional enough just remembering she was gone.

It is amazing how the mind works. I could not believe seeing this image of me standing there with tears running down my face, in my heart I knew they were for grandma. I do know this was the first time I experienced someone I loved very much die.

Watching this unfold in my dream, to my surprise my memory of that morning came back to me. Why it took so long for it to surface, I cannot answer that. Maybe my mind had some type of a safety valve to protect me from mentally breaking down. It was usual; never did I experience anything like that before, it was so vivid I knew it was not my imagination. I know the trigger was Dad talking about grandma today.

However, what was strange to me mom and Dad never said anything to us about that morning incident. Never were we given any details about her death, even when we were older, I guess they figured it was best to leave well enough alone, since there were other issues they never wanted to reveal. Even though I remembered grandma's death, which made me sad all over again, it also brought back memories of my early childhood, since it was around that same period.

In the past, whenever we adults would sit around and reminisce about our early years, the good old days, I would always get upset, because all I remembered were bits and pieces of that time in my life. Since I was the oldest, I always expected myself to remember everything. Now, I can say I do, and that makes me thrilled.

I was amazed when I saw the neighborhood and the house I grew up in, it felt like I was living there all over again. I could see all my friends, to me it felt like I was watching TV it was so real. I would not have changed a thing.

What a special neighborhood our parents raised us in. Most of our neighbors were Catholic families. To us kids, that only meant one thing, many kids to play with. For us, life was great. With having, seven brothers and sisters there was always enough chaos in the household to keep mom on her toes.

My Dad was a very hard worker. He knew having eight children was not going to be financially easy but we never went without. He was very demanding to himself and to us. When we got older I remember how he stressed the fact everyone needed a college education, more so with the boys than the girls. Dad himself was still working on his College degree at the University of Detroit in Michigan, along with working long hours while mom was left holding down the fort.

In my mind, we were a perfect example of a close-knit family. I guess you could have compared us to the "Leave it to Beaver show, the Cleaver's," only with more kids. Always there was respect and obedience in our household at all times. If we even thought about looking at our parents in the wrong way they grounded us; it was worse than timeout that parents use today.

I have to say, having a big family meant to me two things, never a dull moment, and many funny and sad memories to share. For me, the funny ones I will always cherish, but the sad ones, will remain only shadows in my mind, which became the trigger for my dream that night.

Remembering one of my family's funniest episodes, even to this day always makes me laugh. Most of the time they centered around Rick and Bob, my younger brothers, and the situations they always managed to get in trouble with. This particular incident happened when they were a little older, about seven and eight. Really, age did not matter with them they were always getting into trouble.

With Dad working long hours, poor mom was the one that had to do the disciplining. The way she had to handle it was definitely a challenge for her, because Rick and Bob never stood still. Whenever they knew they were in trouble, they would always take off running from mom. If there was going to be any disciplining, she had to catch them first and boy could they run fast.

Since I was not the one in trouble, although I was the one that caused them to get into trouble by telling on them, I just sat back and watched the show. It looked like this funny skit from a circus. As soon as they realized they had pushed mom to the limit, especially when they heard me yell, "mom, the boys are at it again," off they went trying to run from her.

Their favorite spot to run to was this huge oval dinning room table, and always the furthest side away from mom. In their minds, thinking mom could not reach them, so they were safe. As they stood there daring her to come running after them, then the minute she got close, they would take off running around the table again.

This went on back and forth for a while until mom's frustration became so bad all she could say, while trying to catch her breath no less was, "boys you're just making this worse, I'm getting very mad." Causing her to get mad enough to bring out her only defensive weapon of choice, the **"broom,"** by now, she was an expert on using it. In her mind, it was easier for her to reach them across the table with the broom, giving them a hardy swat at the same time, than running after them all day long.

Watching this show, you could see her trying to swing the broom, although every time she did, she would miss and hit the table; all that did was start everyone laughing, even mom. The boys were becoming very good at ducking, causing the laughter to get louder, by this time mom was steaming mad, even though she was still trying to hide her laughter. That's all she needed, then all hell broke out, which was your clue to run for cover because out came those scary words, **"just wait until your father gets home."** Those were frightening words in our household, which always sent us into a panic. It was like the straw that broke the camel back, mom being the camel. Luckily, for us, when Dad finally got home from work most of the time we were in bed for the night, by then moms frustrations had passed. **Thank goodness.**

Looking back at our first house was amazing. I could not believe how small it was. Having one bathroom with a big family must have been a challenge for everyone. It really seemed smaller when my uncle, who was Dad's only sibling and his family came to live with us. Dad being older of the two boys was always there for his brother, helping him out whenever he could. Their family needed a place to stay for a while so in they came with two more kids. Eventually they got back on their feet and found a place of their own.

CHAPTER 6
Was A.L.S. the cause grandma's death?

It wasn't very long after my uncle and his family moved out, that my grandmother, my Dad's mom, and my step grandfather moved in with us. I bet mom and Dad felt like they had a revolving door. I was excited with them moving in, even though it meant I had to give up my bedroom on the first floor for grandma and grandpa to use, I didn't care.

The worst thing I had to deal with was moving upstairs with my two brothers. We shared this huge divided attic; the girls were in one large room and the boys in the other. Although I had to walk through the boys room to go downstairs, as they threw pillows at me telling me to get out of their room. All of that I tolerated because my grandma was here to live with us.

My brothers were excited also. Not just for grandma but her dog that came with her. In a way, grandma's dog became our very first pet. Even though Dad was not excited to have a dog in the house, he soon got used to it. In fact, through the years we managed to have two more dogs in our life. I guess he was a push over when it came to us kids.

Regrettably, when grandma and grandpa moved in with us it was for all the wrong reasons. We, being kids, had no idea that grandma was getting very sick and grandpa needed more help with caring for her. I remember her being in a wheelchair all the time. Only being six years old, it was hard for me to understand why she could not walk.

Our Dad never went into too many details about her, it was something us kids just got used to, you know how kids are; they don't pay any attention to things like that.

Except for me, I was the one with the inquisitive mind, always asking all kinds of questions. Probably to the point that it was very annoying to mom and Dad, but I never let up. Nevertheless, the only thing that mattered to me was my loving grandma was here with us and in my eyes to stay forever.

When I fell asleep, my dream took me back to that time in my life, it felt good seeing my past, and it truly gave me a lot of comfort. Even though I must have blocked out grandma's death, I was still fortunate to remember all the wonderful experiences that I shared with her. In a little girl's eyes, this happy memory truly left an impression on me, helping grandma make cakes. Even to this day, when I smell a cake baking I think of her.

I remember feeling very proud of the fact that I could put the cake in the oven, of course with supervision. I was a great helper to my grandma; my job was to get all the bowls and pans out for her. Being in a wheelchair it was hard for her to do. Knowing grandma's hands hurt a lot, I would help her stir the batter; I certainly did not want to see her in pain. Of course, everyone knows that the best part of making a cake was licking the bowl. To my excitement, I never had to share with my two brothers. They were not even interested in the cake until it was ready to eat, then you had to hide part of it or it would have been all gone at one time.

Then one day for some reason, no **more cakes.** Grandma's hands started to lose their strength and eventually gave out. Shortly after that, she was unable to get out of bed anymore. That bothered me the most. I could not understand why she did not want to get up anymore and make cakes with me. In my young mind, I was wondering if she was mad at me. I knew she still had a wheelchair, so why didn't she want to use it? She could not even hold a book in her hands anymore to read to me.

I always worried that maybe I did something wrong to hurt her feelings, to the point I could actually feel my heart breaking. Mom tried her best to reassure me that was not the case. She kept on reassuring me that grandma loved me very much but she was very sick.

I still have this vision of my mom caring for grandma, feeding her as if she was a little baby. To me it really looked strange because grandma was a big person. After awhile my parents didn't allow us to go into her bedroom anymore, never fully understanding why, left a huge void in my heart.

I cannot imagine how much stress that was for mom. Not only was she tending to grandma's needs, but also she had a young family to care for at the same time. Of course, to us it just looked like part of mom's normal every day routine with her chores. Never did we think grandma was dying. Shortly after grandma moved in with us, she passed away. I was very upset for a long time because I did not have enough time with her.

When I remember that complete scenario that morning, it's no wonder it could traumatize a little child. My dream felt so real I actually felt like I was right there at that exact moment.

I saw myself getting up for breakfast that morning to go downstairs. However, I always had to go through my brother's room to get to the stairs. As I walked quietly by their beds, I glanced over to see if they were still sleeping. To my surprise, mom was in bed with them with her arms wrapped tightly around them. What I did not realize, earlier that morning, grandpa came to mom and Dad's room to wake them telling them grandma had just died. I think Mom coming upstairs to cuddle with the boys was her way of comfort for her grief, also to stop us before we went downstairs. I know she felt it would have been too traumatizing for us to see grandma dead in her room. Her plan was to keep us upstairs until grandma was out of the house. Nevertheless, it backfired on her.

When I saw mom in bed with the boys, I knew something was up. I asked her "why she was up here", all she said was, "I wanted to talk to you kids about your grandma." Well that certainly did not work for me, all that did was spark my curiosity, after all, we were all hungry for breakfast, and it was time for me to go to school. Anyway, I figured she could talk to us down stairs after we went to the bathroom and said good morning to grandma, which was always my routine I got used to doing after they moved in with us. Even if I woke them both up I did not care, I needed a hug and kiss before my day started.

Down we went with mom following behind us insisting we go straight to the kitchen to eat breakfast first. Thinking this is strange, as I said to mom, "we never did that before, and you know our kitchen table is too small for all of us. Besides," I said to mom, "we have to use the bathroom first." Mom tried so hard to avoid that because grandma's bedroom was just down the hall. She knew, at least I was going to run into her room to say good morning. Racing down the hall to the bathroom yelling and pushing each other out of the way to see who was going to use the bathroom first, just like everything else in my family always a race to be the first I never noticed grandma's door was closed.

All of sudden I looked towards the front door and saw Dad standing there as if he was waiting for someone to come, which was strange to me because he was always gone to work before we got up.

Mom tried to hustle us back in to the kitchen before I noticed grandma's bedroom door being closed, but it was too late. It was then mom had to tell us grandma had just died. Trying to explain to us why we need to stay in the kitchen and out of the way until this big white van came to take her away. All that did was start a lot of chaos. I started crying and yelling at the same time **"what happened to my grandma, what do you mean she died?"** There was no way we understood what death meant, we never experienced it before.

Just at that moment a strange feeling came over me, I knew I was not going to see my grandma ever again. I could not stop yelling. **"Mom,"** I said, **"I want to see my** grandma, **I haven't said good morning to her yet, why does she want to leave us?"**

Mom tried to calm me down while still standing in the archway of the kitchen blocking our view of the hallway where grandma's bedroom was. She was fearful that we were too young to handle what was going to happen next. I could not stand it trying hard to push mom out of the way so I could peak through her legs to see what was going

39

All of a sudden, I saw Dad opening the door directing these two men with this tall bed with wheels down the hall to grandma's room. If only I was not this inquisitive little girl what I saw next put me in a state of shock it is no wonder I blocked it out of my memory.

Standing there wondering and waiting for those men to come out of grandma's room felt like hours. The reality was it was seconds. Still battling with mom, I pushed her out of my way so I could see clearly grandma's bedroom door opened up. Out came these two men pushing my grandma on this bed with her head all covered up. All I could do was cry and yell at the top of my lungs. "**Where are you going with my grandma bring her back why are you letting them take her mom she's my grandma leave her here!!!**" I could not stop yelling I wanted so bad to run after her, but mom didn't let me!

Then as I looked over at Dad still not understanding what was going on hoping he would help me I started yelling at him "**Daddy stop those men. Why do they have grandma's face covered up? My grandma cannot breathe. Please Daddy don't let grandma go out the door I haven't said goodbye.**"

As mom tried to calm me down trying to explain what death meant I could feel the tears running down my cheek. All I could see were mom's lips moving but no words were coming out. **I know I was in shock, all I wanted was my grandma back but that never happened.**

Of course, realizing as I woke up this was not a dream it truly was my imbedded memories coming back. I even found my pillow all wet from the tears that were dripping down my face as I remembered that night.

The reality was her cause of death remained a mystery to Dad and mom. They had to keep their fears of the unknown illness to themselves especially for our sake. Yes, they had the death certificate stating the cause of death **heart attack** but the fear of other health issues was always there.

Even though Dad may have felt there were health issues in the family it wasn't until many years later when we were at the Mayo Clinic for Dad's illness did we realize grandma's condition was likely to have been some type of a neurological disorder. Because of Dad's A.L.S. diagnosis, the doctors speculated this to be hereditary, hence solving grandma's diagnosis. Dad never knew what it was or even worse, how severe it was going to affect our family. If he had any idea at all after grandma's death, he would have never had four more kids.

I vaguely remember being at my grandma's funeral. There were a lot of aunts and uncles there I never met. Even some of the older relatives Dad hardly knew. The funeral home was very interesting to me. Everyone was there to see grandma. I could not figure out why because her eyes were not open and she could not talk. To me it felt like this huge party, especially with all the family around.

Being an inquisitive child I would love to listen to the conversation's the adults were having but that did not last long. As soon as mom and Dad caught me they told me to leave the room. Always telling me this was grownup talk. Of course, that only sparked my curiosity to sneak back in when they were not watching. Never did I understand any of their conversations all they seem to want to talk about was grandma's leg problems.

Over and over I kept on hearing the words "leg problem" which was very puzzling to me. I could not understand why grandma's legs were such a concern to them. I remember seeing my Dad in the room as he mingled from one relative to another always with this concerned look on his face. I knew it was his worry face because I saw it many times before.

What was odd to me I never remembered bringing up her death when I was older. All I could remember about that time in my life was the good things I did with her. The way she died never surfaced again for me, which always surprised my mom and Dad since I was so inquisitive…. until the night in my dream.

As I started to wake up my dream began to fade away I realized it was daylight and it was time to be with my family. They left me alone all night. I know it was good for me but now I needed them. Realizing it was going to be their love and support to help me through Dad's illness.

Even though I finally remembered my grandma's death, which made me sad all over again, it also made me feel grateful for all the fond memories that took me back to that time in my life. I cannot tell you how much comfort that gave me because of that; I knew I was prepared to face anything.

Although, still wondering in the back of my mind if remembering grandma's death was actually true or maybe it was only a figment of my imagination just to give me comfort. I had to find out. Only one person who could help me was mom.

The next day when I saw her and told her about my dream the look on her face told me everything. **"Wow"** she said with surprise, "I can't believe that yes it happened just like you said. Did Dad ever say anything to you about that experience? You never had any questions when you were younger, which we knew you never held back with those. Dad and I figured none of you kids remembered seeing anything. Since you were so young, we just left it alone. "I can't tell you how many times I tried to prepare myself to answer that question especially the older you got. Eventually the subject just faded away."

You know I sometimes wondered if our dreams are only our deepest inner thoughts trying to find a way to surface and for some unknown reason it only happens when we are mentally ready to face them. After remembering all of this, I was thankful that mom was here to verify everything for me. I had to make sure I was not **dreaming and I did remember after all.**

CHAPTER 7
The Second Generation Growing

Many years had gone by since grandma's death. It was now 1964, four of us were teenagers and the other four were 8-6-5 and 3 years old. I always found it strange the way mom and Dad ended up with five years between the two groups of siblings. Linda the youngest of the first four and Ray the youngest of the second four. We never could figure out why there was such a big gap in between. Maybe mom just needed a break or maybe she was just crazy and wanted a second family that's exactly how it felt growing up, two different families.

I know mom was Catholic and had very strong beliefs when it came to birth control. In those days within the Catholic faith, the type of birth control recommended was the rhythm system. If you were of Catholic faith, you would understand what it was. Even though Dad was raised Baptist which he never practiced, I found it comical when he said, "when it came to birth control he was very good at accommodating mom with this particular belief." We all chuckled and said, yep that's our Dad.

Through the years with having eight children they were grateful there was never any serious health problems to cope with. The only family crisis we ever had to deal with was the death of an aunt or uncle or a grandparent. That's life and everyone goes through it. If it was a parent well—that is a different story. I could not imagine having to deal with that.

Now and then, I remember having feelings about how nice it was not to have any family crisis to go through. Even thinking my parents would live forever. I know that was a little far fetched but the reality was I never gave their death any thought. I know with a large family like ours the odds were very strong that somewhere along our road there probably would have been some type of a serious incident for us to handle. Thank God, it never happened—at least not at this point.

I always had thoughts of maybe our lives were too good to be true we were a very lucky and blessed family. Having those feelings crossing my mind now and then made me fearful to share it with anyone thinking somehow I would jinx my thoughts and something would happen to change them.

In1965, I have to say was an exciting year for Dad and I. His career was going strong with Ford Motor Company, and was climbing the ladder and on his way to great endeavors. Myself I was turning17 and entering the 12th grade and met the love of my life my future husband Jim.

Everything was going great until Dad decided to move the family in my senior year no less from the city to the suburbs. It was devastating for me because Jim and I ended up at different high schools in our senior year. Thinking the distance would end our relationship made me feel like it was the end of the world. Remarkably as faith would have it, we stayed together and married in February 1966 just 7 months after graduation.

The circle of life was now starting with the second generation. In May 1967, mom and Dad were becoming grandparents for the first time. Jim and I had our first daughter Kimberly. It was hard for mom to be too excited because she still had three of my younger siblings at home my brother Ray being the youngest was only 6 when Kim was born. He was the wild one and insanely jealous of the new arrival in the family. Even though Kim was not around all the time, he still did not like having the center of attention taken away from him.

In March 1966, Jim received his draft notice. After basic training and MOS school in April, Jim ended up in Taiwan. Kimberly was two months old before we were able to join him. I will never forget how devastated mom was. This was the first time anyone in the family moved away. Not only did we move out of the state but out of the country.

Vietnam was going hot and heavy and the odds were Jim was heading there. Thank God, he enlisted for another year and took advantage of going to MOS school because it kept him from going to Vietnam. Still moving away was not easy for mom or I. However, who could say no to the Army.

Living in Taiwan was completely different from the States. At the time, the States were ten years ahead of Vietnam with our culture. It certainly was a lifetime experience. Being only 19, I was too young to appreciate it. Thank God, I was with my husband all that time. If I were living with my parents until Jim got home mom would have gone crazy with me moping around all the time.

Not coming back to the states for a couple of years especially with having the first grandchild was tremendously hard for mom. Watching Kim grow through all those precious moments made me sad that grandma could not enjoy it. She was two and half when Jim's army duty was over from then on she became mom's favorite. Of course, grandma never admitted to that but it was obvious. Until her little Renée came along my Sister Mary's little girl. By then Kim was a young adult.

When Jim and I returned to the states, it was time to find a home near them again. There was never any questions asked from my husband he just knew it was important for me.

I have to say it was strange no one else in the family moved away especially starting their own careers. With such a large family, the chance of that happening was very good. Everyone was fortunate to find work in Michigan.

I have heard there is always a reason for why things happen the way they do. Many years later when Dad became ill, I realized it was meant to be. If it were not for the family, being together and pulling together it would have been impossible for us to handle his illness.

It did not seem very long until there were three more weddings in the family. The birth of the grandkids was growing by leaps and bounds four more to be exact. Of course, mom and Dad were a long way from being finished with grandkids. Life for our family was flowing very smoothly still not having any idea what was lurking in our shadows.

I cannot imagine being in Dad's shoes knowing that now mom and he were having grandchildren and if there was a threat of a family disease, you now had the third generation being involved. The unknowing must have been a tremendous burden. It had to be unbearable for him at times. It was amazing he never showed it even when we were adults, there were never any clues how could there be we were not aware something was seriously wrong.

In writing this story and visualizing this unfolding all over again it is easier to see how Dad actually carried all that weight on his shoulders for many years. At the time, we blamed the uptight attitude on having a bad day with work never giving it a second thought that maybe something else might be bothering him.

CHAPTER 8
After Germany, life and career back on track

In the mid 70s, Dad took a promotion transferring him to Germany working for Ford of Europe. With his new position, he was in charge of all car engineering in Europe. Mom and my four younger siblings went with him. What a catastrophe it was when Dad told us Ford Motor Company wanted him to move to Germany. The family felt like it was the end of the world. I know in the past they asked him to make a transfer but he was always able to turn them down without a risk of job security. Never did we give it much thought it would happen again. The reality was mom did not want to leave the rest of her family especially with the four oldest now having families. Leaving her grandkids behind was hard but this time she had no choice.

The four youngest were still in school three in high school the other one close behind. Leaving all their friends behind definitely caused a lot of chaos. I know it was the beginning of my sister Sue rebelling.

It was hard adjusting to mom and Dad being in Germany. With our family being big on traditions, birthdays, Father's day, Mother's day, Christmas, we were always together. However, not to have Sunday dinners for a while well that was a very different story. I guess the four families that were still at home could have carried on with the tradition but it was not the same without them. To us this was our first major family crisis we had to face. Dad knew everyone was having a hard time with this move especially mom. Unfortunately, this time his hands were tied and could not turn this down.

The Company needed Dad to head up a new program in Europe, and in turn, they promised bigger plans for him when he returned to the States. So with a ***LOT*** of resistance, mom and four younger kids all packed up and moved. Mom was very lonely over there dad's working hours were more demanding. Being lonely for the rest of her children and grandkids that were home is why Dad made sure the rest of us took turns coming to Germany for vacations. It was very important for him to keep mom happy and being around her kids was her happiest times.

When it was my family's turn to go there, Jim was on temporary layoff from Ford Motor Company. It was the first major layoff Ford went through back in the 70s. My brother Bob and his family were living in an apartment and were looking to buy a home so they offered to move in our house until we came home.

We were able to spend six weeks in Europe it was wonderful. What great therapy it was for mom and the four younger siblings. Dad took a lot of vacation time and we traveled throughout Europe. It felt like a fairy tale vacation the best part it was all free. I know we would have stayed longer but Jim received his notice to go back to work.

My brother Bob and his family were ready to move because they bought a home just a couple blocks away from us. It could not have worked out better for everyone. Even though we were fortunate to have mom and Dad come home every Christmas, with them being gone for three years still felt like an eternity for us.

While in Germany a situation they encountered with Ron who was a senior in high school at the time scared mom and Dad. Which I didn't understand why they were so concerned because this wasn't the first time one of us kids was hospitalized. Ron was complaining a lot about leg pain, to the point that it started to interfere with his walking. I remember mom's phone call from Germany explaining to me about Ron's situation.

When she told me what had happened I could tell she was on the verge of revealing something else that was on her mind. The sound in her voice was strange. Before she finished there was a long silence on the phone. It was as if she was trying hard not to cry. I kept on asking mom is Ron was all right. With a deep sigh, she finally said, "yes now everything is fine honey thank goodness."

As she explained further telling me that, the doctor found a small tumor in his leg that was pressing on a nerve, which was causing problems with his walking. They did minor surgery and he was just fine. She told me how aggressive Dad was trying to find the best doctor for Ron. I could not imagine him being in such a panic mode it never was in his nature to do that. I am sure it worried the family. It's was strange though, I do remember mom accidentally saying to me that Dad felt there was something else going on with Ron although at the time I did not question her.

After that phone call with mom, I told Jim if mom felt it was important for me to know something she would have shared it with me then. Of course, that never happened so I tried to let it go. The important thing was Ron was fine and he was able to graduate with his class. He never seemed to have any more problems at least not until many years later.

I do believe as I write my thoughts down on paper knowing what the family health secret is all about now, when mom called me that day to tell me about Ron there is no doubt in my mind she was very close to revealing that secret to me right then.

We were all excited when they came home from Germany. It was as if they were never gone. Family traditions were back on track. Even though Dad's work still kept him very busy that wasn't new to us we were just glad they were home.

Ford kept their word. Dad was responsible with a new important project. You could tell this one was very different from all the other ones he worked on before he was like a little kid anticipating Christmas. With Dad's new responsibility, keeping him very busy it was important that we went back to our Sunday dinners. At least we were back enjoying that again.

I tried to imagine mom cooking those diners for our large family and was always amazed how she managed to do it. I think she was in the kitchen all day. Now dinner was first come first serve since the family was so large. We use to have dinner around the dining room table before we got so big now every meal was a buffet. One of the most popular dishes in the family was mash potatoes. If you were not first in line, they were gone before you got to them. I guess that is one of the consequences of having a large family.

By this time, there were 10 grandkids and our family was still growing. We still had three siblings who were not married yet. Ray 24, Sue 25, and fussy brother Ron 27, back then 27 was old not to be married. I guess that is why we called him fussy. Ron was always looking for the perfect girl. He finally found Kim about a year later was married and eventually had three beautiful children.

Ron, Sue, and oldest brother Rick followed in Dad footsteps and worked at Ford Motor Company. My Husband Jim did also. I guess you could say Ford Motor Company ran in our blood.

The youngest brother Ray did not have a particular job. He was always around the house helping mom out. Since mom never had a driver's license Ray took her everywhere. I know mom was spoil with all that attention.

Ray was the youngest sibling in the family her baby. Maybe that is why she was not ready for him to leave home. He was company for her and at the same time security when Dad was out of town. There were many arguments between mom and Dad about Ray not working or going to college. Dad was always very demanding with that. If you did not have a job, you had better had plans for college or you were going in the service. However, for some reason mom would always win the argument. It never happened with the other three boys. Who would have guessed that it was probably fate that kept him home because we soon found out when Dad got ill how much he needed Ray's help.

CHAPTER 9

When Dad's fears became stronger, so did his quest to find answers

Without us knowing, Dad was starting to have strange symptoms within his body he never felt before. Now as I write my thoughts down I can clearly see the panic starting to grow inside him as he secretly started searching out answers to help solve this family health puzzle. It seems all the pieces were finally coming together unfortunately; it took me 22 years to realize it. Still to this day, I probably would not have paid any attention to that issue if I were not writing this book. Even if I knew about a hereditary illness before I got married I do not think it would have changed my life. I cannot imagine not having Jim and my two daughters in it, even worse life without grandkids!

To this day I cannot imagine how Dad kept his fears to himself especially the older we became. He did a great job of hiding it because we never knew anything until that somber day at our Sunday dinner. I do not know if I could have been as strong as he was.

Now with the family starting to grow, especially the third generation, the fear of himself becoming ill only made the quest stronger to find some facts to back up this unknown illness. How hard was that to do and at the same time not alarm any of us? The clues were always there especially when he did things out of character. However, who was looking for them. We had no idea anything was wrong. I have to admit no matter what happen with this secrete it would not have changed the inevitable.

Looking back, I remember all the ways Dad tried to seek out relatives he never stayed in touch with at the time I thought it was very strange. Thinking to myself maybe, he is just getting sentimental in his older age. He never was the type to keep in touch. It was hard enough keeping up with us.

Dad only had one sibling a brother, although growing up they were close to a few cousins and an aunt who was on his Dad's side of the family. Unfortunately, after his brother died for some reason Dad lost touch with them.

Mom used to talk about a relationship between Dad's father and his uncle. For some unexplainable reasons it took a turn for the worse when Dad was away in the Navy she never went into details.

Dad was a very private man and did not share much of his past with us. He did now and then spoke about Aunt Mae. She and grandma were good friends especially after she married into the family. I know Dad would get a Christmas card from Aunt Mae every year, which always got my attention. I remember asking mom who she was and why we have not we met her. Of course always ending up with the same story the family split up.

One day Dad received a card from his aunt Mae saying his uncle Melvin died his dad's brother. She was letting him know that she was going to be at his funeral and would love to see him. I found it very odd that he agreed to go since it was this side of the family that had this disagreement. It certainly made me wonder why he was so anxious to see her after all those years.

Mom, Jim, and I went along with him. It was the first time I met any of his side of the family. To me all I could remember was Aunt Mae was quite old. Mom told me later grandma would have been the same age if she were still alive.

The whole time we were at the funeral it looked like she and Dad had a lot of catching up to do. It seemed like he talked to no one else but his aunt Mae. It is easy for me to see now he was trying to find out more information on grandma's health. Since the two of them were close, maybe she could have helped him solved his mystery. I think that day he finally confided in someone about his fears. Whether she was able to satisfy his quest, we never found out. I do know one thing the ride home that afternoon was very quiet.

It is easy for me to see now how Dad's haunting thoughts of what really took grandma's life was truly bothering him even more, especially when his symptoms became stronger. His mind constantly occupied with stress and it was not just from work. There were many questions needing answers, but all his avenues for information were fading away. To know how to go about seeking them out without causing another panic in the family was hard for him to do.

It is amazing how things turned out for us, as if grandma was guiding Dad in this direction. You see a couple of days after this funeral Dad received a card in the mail from his uncle's family inviting all of us to his uncle's surprise birthday party. He was grandma's brother whom we never knew. I had a feeling Dad himself was surprised he was still living. It certainly surprised us since Dad never spoke about him.

His uncle was turning 80 and when Dad read the card, he was excited to go to their party and wanted all of us to go with him. To me that was out of character for Dad to respond in that way he certainly wasn't a mingle type of a family Man. In the end, it did not matter because we treated this like a family weekend trip.

It was nice to see relatives I did not know I had. Although again just like the last time with his Aunt Mae the whole time we were there all Dad did was talk to his uncle. I can still envision them in deep conversation which lasted late into the night. Of course, at that time I never derived a conclusion I just thought he was excited to see him, and was missing the good old days.

Looking back, I know Dad was there for more than his uncle's birthday party. It was the same feeling I got when we went to his Uncle Melvin's funeral. He was trying to find some answers to the family health history.

Yes, I am sure it was nice for him to see relatives that he had not seen in a long time however I know Dad thought for sure he was going to get some answers about what grandma died from after all his uncle was grandma's brother.

It was not until much later when we were at the Mayo Clinic for Dad's second opinion that I realized he never got any information from his uncle. If he did, he would have shared it with the doctors. On the other hand, maybe he did and still did not want us to know until the doctors confirmed his diagnosis. Whatever the case was, it still left us in the dark.

As usual it did not seem to bother Dad too long because his mind went right back on track with life. That was that type of man he was. Since there was nothing he could do at this point, he decided not to worry about things he had no control over. Dad always had a level attitude with everything he dealt with. I am sure that was one of his special characteristic of his personality, which also helped in work.

My Dad became very successful, not only with work but also with family life. It is amazing how he kept everything together even with the weight of his health on his mind. Dad's achievements and determination with his hard work were finally paying off. Unfortunately, his fears of the mysterious health secret were getting stronger and stronger also. What a nightmare for him to be facing. It just did not seem fair. It was as if he was shot down in the prime of his life.

Finally, Dad's doctor appointment was here. It seemed like an eternity since that day in their kitchen when he shared his fears with us. We were all very glad he was finally going. The unknown was becoming harder for all of us to deal with.

I could not wait to hear what the doctor was going to tell Dad. Because I was so anxious I went over to their house to wait with mom, at least I felt I was doing something constructive, comforting mom. She did not ask why I was there just grateful I was.

Thank goodness, my kids were in school. I know they would have sensed I was worried about something, which would have been very hard to explain since I did not know myself.

I am not sure if I was company for mom all I did when I got there was pace back and forth from the window to the door. In my mind, thinking maybe if I got a glance at the expression on Dad's face before he came in the door it would have prepared me for whatever he had to tell us. I was so nervous, which was the weirdest thing because I did not know why. Although, it was obvious to mom what was going on still she never confided in me.

My mind was going out of control with frightening thoughts trying to figure out what was happening. One thing I did know for sure it was serious Dad never acted like this before. Since they already told us something was happening with his health, all this waiting only made me feel uptight.

It seemed like forever until Dad came home. When he pulled in the driveway, my heart sank. As soon as mom saw his car, she started crying. When Dad got out of the car, I tried to read the expression on his face. It astounded me his complexion was ghostly color. My heart was beating a 100 miles an hour. When he came in the door, he did not say a thing to mom or me he just went straight into the kitchen and sat down. I remember standing there waiting for him to say something just anything praying everything was going to be ok.

Suddenly he let out this big sigh and proceeded to tell us what the doctor's diagnosis was. As he explained to us, I could see this tremendous relief in his eyes. He said the problem in his leg was from an inflammation called phlebitis with antibiotics it would run its course and in time would get better. Mom and I just looked at each other and started crying. Mom's cry was from relief mine I did not understand why I was crying however, there was no doubt, our tears were happy ones. When I glanced towards mom and Dad I saw them staring at each other. I had a weird feeling they thought it was going to be a different diagnosis the relief in their eyes was obvious.

Unfortunately, this was just the beginning of Dad's nightmare. The antibiotics the doctor gave him for his symptoms were not working. I cannot tell you how many times our emotions went up and down throughout his ordeal. Back to the doctor he went. This time the doctor decided to send him to a Vascular Surgeon. Telling him it might be a circulatory disorder a cyst or even a blood clot that may have ruptured at the back of his leg.

When they did an ultrasound, it turned out negative. As the doctor proceeded to tell Dad about the results, again there was this huge sigh of relief. Although I had a feeling, he was hoping his leg pain would have been as simple as that. The doctor recommended he wait to see if there were any more flare-ups before he continued with any more testing.

We were all relieved because in our eyes it looked like the doctor was not too concerned about his condition maybe it was not as serious as we thought. We could have been blowing this all out of proportion. We had a tendency to do that.

However, I could tell Dad still was not satisfied with the doctor's decision he knew something was not right. Nevertheless, until there was a definite diagnosis we all tried to continue with our lives and for now we were very grateful Dad were all right. At least we had that to hang on to for a little while.

CHAPTER 10
Our family trip was the first scare with Dad's health, Global Amnesia

After that visit, mom and dad started to act very strange. Mom mentioned that Dad wanted to take a family weekend trip. He wanted everyone to go and the treat was on him. He said it would be fun for all of us to be together like a mini vacation.

That in itself was very strange for Dad. Most of the time his weekends were down time he needed the relaxation especially with his busy workweek. Mom always had to twist his leg for him to spend the money on something like this especially with our large family.

I can clearly see how his desire to be around the family more started to become his first choice and for the first time, work came in second. At the time I did not give it a second thought it was fun just going along. I figured I might as well "milk it" as long as it lasted.

Our getaway was to a family indoor resort in Canada. The grandkids thought it was great going to another country, which was very easy to do living in Michigan.

The resort had indoor pool game rooms and all kinds of activities for the kids to do. All our rooms were poolside, which made you feel like you were sitting on a beach in the middle of winter. The dinners together were awesome. Unfortunately, the only restaurant they had besides a hamburger joint was fine dining. This still worked out great because Dad taught the grandkids to appreciate the fine taste of escargot. As he encouraged them to try escargot, to his surprise they loved it. That is all grandpa needed. He then let them order as much as they wanted. The funny part was when it came time to order the main meal all they wanted was hamburgers and French fries. We always laughed at that combination. That night our kids acquired the taste for fine dining! **(Thanks a lot Dad!)**

Even though we were all having a great time we also experienced our first serious scare with Dad's health, which totally freaked us out. It was shortly after dinner when we were walking back to our rooms. Dad said he was not feeling good and wanted to go to bed. Although, going to bed early was normal for him. However, what bothered me was the fact Dad said he did not feel good. He was very cautious with telling us, he knew we had a tendency to panic. This time was different I think he was warning us something was not right with him, which really made me feel uneasy.

Since all our rooms were poolside and close together it made it easy for me to monitor the kids swimming as I paced back and forth by his room. I was very protective of my Dad; I think all daughters are that way.

When I went to bed that night I could not sleep. I think I tossed and turned most of the night, which was very unusual for me because I never had any problems sleeping. My mind was going in circles hoping there was nothing wrong with Dad.

All of a sudden, we heard this loud knock on the door it was mom in a panic yelling for us. "I need help there is something seriously wrong with Dad come quickly." We rushed over to his room and found Dad sitting on the edge of the bed just staring into space. He did not know where he was or who we were. I was so scared! I never saw my Dad like that before. The first thing that crossed my mind was Dad had a stroke. That's when I remember grandma's stroke that everyone said she had. We were always told that is what she died from, which made me panic even more. Could the same thing happen to Dad as it did to grandma? My mind was racing. I was in a panic stage. Poor Jim he had a hard time trying to get me to settle down so he could tend to Dad.

We hurriedly woke up the rest of the adults knowing together we could figure out what to do. One choice was to go home but that meant waking up all the kids and traveling for three hours. We were too scared to take that chance. We knew the right decision was to take Dad to the hospital right away but being in a different country made you feel leery not knowing what to expect with their health care. Thank goodness, the hotel was so helpful they put us at ease right away.

Some of us went to the hospital the rest stayed in the hotel with the kids. We did not want to wake them for they would have been very frightened to see grandpa in that condition. I do not remember who else went along with Jim and me; all I remember was no one was going to keep me back. In my mind, I knew I could take better care of Dad than anyone else could.

What a quiet ride it was! I remember when Jim started to drive to the hospital not knowing if we were going in the right direction. Making a comment loudly with a panic in his voice he said, "I can't find a hospital sign." All of a sudden, as if Dad was coming out of his trance he spoke up, "there's a sign over there it's pointing that way." Which was very strange because as fast as he spoke up he went back into his trance the same way and never said anything else. He just continued to have this blank look on his face.

When we arrived at the hospital, the doctors checked him out all over. I think they too were concerned he had a stroke, but everything was okay. After a short while, he seemed to come out of his trance and started to recognize everyone.

I still envision myself standing by his bed and asking him all kinds of questions saying repeatedly, "What is your name? Do you know where you are? Do you know who I am?" I think he got tired of hearing it because all of a sudden he said in a very assertive tone in his voice **"now who do you think I am PAM!"** That started all of us laughing with relief. After that, I knew he was going to be fine.

Nevertheless, the only diagnosis we received from the doctors that day was Dad had a case of Global Amnesia with no other explanation and sent him home. They never explained to us what in the world it was. We were okay with that because we had our Dad back to normal.

Thank goodness, the kids were not aware of what happened. When we got back to the hotel, they were just getting up. They never suspected a thing. To them it was a fun weekend. All the way home I was very quiet, I have a tendency to do that when I am worried about something. I just could not shake the terrible feeling something was becoming seriously wrong with Dad's health and this was just the beginning of it.

CHAPTER 11
Preparing for retirement too soon

Shortly after the Canada weekend, Dad started talking about planning for retirement, blaming it on our Michigan winters were starting to get to him. At the time, I thought that was the main reason for sparking his interest to take a trip to Florida. They had friends there and figured it would be a good time to visit them. However, I thought it was strange they were doing this trip so soon after our weekend getaway. Maybe that incident in Canada really scared him, as he realized life was too short and it was time to "stop and smell the roses". The reality was it was out of character for Dad to take much time off work, especially just getting back from Canada. I know mom was probably forcing the issue feeling it was time to start enjoying the family more.

Even though Dad was working on his greatest endeavor for Ford Motor Company, he still wanted everything to be in place when the decision came to retire. To tell you the truth I had a hard time understanding why Dad wanted to retire. I did not think that word was in his vocabulary.

When they came back from Florida, they told us how they fell in love with the beaches there. That's all the convincing they needed, Florida in their mind was the area for retirement. That is when they told us they bought a condominium right on the beach and could not wait for us to see it. Of course, we were all excited however, the thought did cross my mind why that decision was made so fast. I knew my Dad; he was never one to jump the gun on anything especially when money was involved. I have to say it did leave me a little uneasy with all of this planning even though he was doing this for us as well as himself.

Jim said that I had a tendency to worry too much; I guess I have to admit he was right. However, when your parents start to make sure all their retirement finance's are in order, definitely makes you wonder what's wrong. Nevertheless, I tried not to have my thoughts go there, they were not happy ones, and I certainly did not want to jinx myself with negativity. Jim tried to make me realize this was just a smart investment and Dad was only trying to get all his "ducks in a row" for the planning for his wife and children's future.

Still, in my mind what didn't fit this scenario was here was a man who always went 100 miles an hour never slowing down for anything, a man who truly loved his job, and was a picture of health. All of a sudden admitting he was looking at retirement aggressively. No way, he is only 58 and had a lot of knowledge and talent left to give.

What also puzzled me mom was backing him up. I saw how hard it was for her when she moved to Germany, especially not wanting to be away from the rest of the family. Now thinking about staying in Florida even if it was only for the winter months was totally out of character for mom. She was never was one who accepted changes very well. Again, as I told Jim my suspicion he reminded me, "honey your making "mountains out of molehills," just be grateful we can enjoy this with them."

That winter during Christmas break, some of us went to the condominium. Dad took a couple of weeks off work and flew with mom. It was hard for the whole family to go because the condominium only had two bedrooms; our family was just too big. Of course, the only time we could take advantage of doing that in the first place was during holidays because we all had school age children. Nevertheless, we had a hard time convincing the kids we wanted to go for Christmas. Even though they were beyond the age of believing in Santa Claus, to them Christmas was all about snow.

Dad kept telling the kids the beaches were white too, but a lot warmer. He tried to play it up big so they would not say no. He was so funny with all of this, even though it was his idea to go to Florida for Christmas; he pretty much **expected** he was not going to be there alone.

What an effort it was for us to pack up a small car with Christmas presents and drive there. With the kids only having a week off of school we wanted to drive straight through so we had more time to be in Florida, it wasn't that bad, it only took us 24 hours. Now I am glad we did it we enjoyed mom and Dad's company to the fullest. The memories we all shared with them were priceless. You cannot replace fond memories.

It is odd though within a short time frame Dad bought another condominium and a house in Florida. Justifying the buy of our large family. He said it was too hard to choose whose turn it was next for vacations; he never wanted to leave anyone out, and **WAS NOT** going to be alone!

That is when I thought okay, my Dad has really flipped. Was I the only one that was noticing this unusual behavior? Now I realized he was only doing everything he could to make sure his family financially was going to care for. In his eyes these investment secured that. Did Dad have this crystal ball and knew what was ahead for him? Unfortunately, all my questions were answered the day Dad became ill. **However, as I put my thoughts down and re think back to that point in our lives, Dad knew there was something happening to his health the whole time, now it's obvious to see the writing on the wall.**

Although, one thing I did learn about my Dad, he was a very strong-minded person, never was he going to let the fear of uncertainty stop him from doing anything he set his mind to. He proved it with the way he lived his life. Whatever he was suppressing in the back of his mind, he never let it surface. It's amazing how strong willed he was as he tried to shield his children. I could not imagine going through my whole life with that same fear. At least we had some time to adjust before this unknown illness was in our future too.

CHAPTER 12
The ultimate career
Achievement cursed from A.L.S.

Even though Dad was trying to convince everyone he was preparing for retirement, it was obvious he did not want to slow down or even think of leaving his job. In a way it was sad, if it was not for his illness I think we would have had to drag him away from working.

Dad was in the middle of a wonderful career opportunity with Ford Motor Company. You could feel his excitement. It always reminded me of a little kid getting ready to open this huge present. This project Dad was working on turned out to be the most successful car line ever developed in Ford Motor Company history since the Mustang.

OCTOBER 1985

Supercharger
Detroit Section SAE

Wednesday, October 2 — Ford Taurus and Mercury Sable

It was the famous Dual, the Ford Taurus, and The Mercury Sable. Dad was now Chief Engineer of Ford Motor Company large Car Division and Car Design Development. His responsibilities were the engineering and coordination. This new carline represented Ford's most expensive product development program in the North American market at that time, about $3 billion, which now a days seems like chump change.

These in a way were his babies. We were so proud of him and his accomplishments. This was Dad's claim to fame, which for him was the icing on the cake for his career. He should have been able to enjoy this moment to its fullest; instead, it became the beginning of his worst **nightmare**. His family's health secret was no longer a mystery it revealed its ugly face. I sadly remember this incident just like it was yesterday; to me it felt like the end of the world, which it pretty much became for our whole family.

The year was 1985, the Taurus and Sable was getting ready to go into production in Atlanta Georgia where the plant was. Dad and his co-workers were going there to make sure these two car lines were ready for their big launch, one of his many trips. Dad had a hard time controlling his excitement for this trip. It was easy for us to tell because he would go around the house while packing his suitcase snapping his fingers, which was a little quirk he always did when he was extremely excited. It still brings a smile to my face imagining him doing it right now.

What truly was unfair even to this day, which I still have a hard time understanding is why did his excitement of his achievement become cursed with the start of this illness. Can you imagine all in the same day the happiest time in your life brought down with your worst nightmare? This devastating health curse could have struck him later on in his life, why now, it was not fair.

To this day, I still cannot get over the way it happened. It was so fast it made you wonder if he had any warnings and he never wanted us to worry. Yes, we knew he had a leg problem, but we thought that had passed and he was out of the woods, we were not prepared for this nor was Dad, at least I thought so.

Dad arrived at the airport that day with his co-workers and was walking to their gate for departure. He was feeling a little uneasy with his balance. All of a sudden, his feet slipped out from under him and he fell to the floor. It was as if he tripped but nothing was in his way. His friends cautiously got him back on his feet and were very concerned for him. He was a little weak, but shaken. Everyone was puzzled at what had just happened. Not knowing what to do for him, they wanted to take him home, but he insisted on going to Atlanta. He needed to make sure these car lines were ready to go into production. My Dad was the type of man in which nothing was going to get in his way. He was determined to see this project all the way through.

We did not know at the time that this incident was one of the first major signs of his A.L.S. All I can say was thank goodness he was stubborn enough and insisted on going to the plant. A few months later, they launched the Taurus and Sable. Sadly, Dad was too weak to go down to Atlanta and be part of the celebration. Thank God, he at least saw them to that point; at least he was able to take part in his greatest achievement.

I was at their house visiting with mom when she got the phone call from Dad telling her about what happened at the airport. It seemed like he was talking to her for a long time. I could see her eyes water up when she finally answered him. I remember her saying to Dad, "when you get home you need to go back to your doctor and let him know what just happened to you, its time we get to the bottom of this." I could not believe I was hearing that excited conversation coming from mom. Anxiously I said, "what is wrong with Dad?" Mom hung up the phone and proceeded to give me just enough information not to scare me. At that point, I knew it was serious, only I could not imagine what was happening to Dad that could have been so alarming. Never could I have realized what was ahead of us. This was the first time we faced a family crisis like this. Dad was never sick, at least not with anything he couldn't recover from.

I remembered that day as I sat with mom in her kitchen waiting together for Dad to get home from his doctor's appointment. The expression on mom's face as she tried hard to hide her fear from me is an image that even to this day I have a hard time getting out of my mind. Now I know she was afraid Dad was coming down with the same thing grandma had only at that time I had no clue.

Even though I truly believe they never knew what grandma had, it was apparent to mom that Dad was falling into the same pattern. How in the world did they manage to keep this health problem a secret from us all those years? It must have been such a heavy burden for both of them to carry. Deep down inside, I know now they were concerned that this illness, whatever it was, could possibly be hereditary. Nevertheless, they had no proof. Nothing to confirm their fears, they had to go on with their lives. I cannot imagine what was going through Dad's mind as he felt this health crisis was now becoming a reality for him. What a frightening thing for him to be facing… **fearing for him and his children as he faced the biggest fight of his life.**

CHAPTER 13

The biggest battle of Dad's life, as he regrouped his thoughts on the beaches of Florida

After his exam, the doctor told Dad that he was sending him to a neurosurgeon, especially when he remembered Dad telling him of an old back injury from football. "You never know" the doctor said, "there could be some type of a recurring problem that could be causing your leg pain. We're going to get to the bottom of this."

When we admitted Dad to the hospital for more testing, I remember it being a very cold day, February 1985. Seeing Dad lying in a hospital bed was very scary for the whole family to face. Here was our Dad, our man of steel, our rock, to us our **SUPERDAD** looking so helpless. We always felt nothing could slow him down; in our eyes, he was invincible. Now, every time I remember that incident I cannot get that image of him lying in a hospital bed looking so forlorn out of my mind. That was not my Dad!

When the neurosurgeon read Dad's report from his physician, again speculating maybe Dad had lumbar-disc disease, which in fact could very easily be causing his leg problem, especially with him having this on and off pain, bracing Dad, telling him that he could possibly need back surgery to correct it.

Again, my memory of what happened to grandma with her back surgery popped into my mind, since the doctors told her she needed back surgery also to correct her problem too. The scariest part of all that was, I recalled Dad saying she seemed worse afterwards. Couldn't Dad tell he was falling into that same pattern? I was having a hard time understanding why he was actually happy to hear about back surgery.

As Dad went on and on talking about his old football injuries, it looked like he was trying to convince himself that indeed this was his problem. I could hear him say, "For as long as I can remember I always had back troubles, I think the doctor has found the answer," releasing a big sigh of relief at the same time.

I know we all have a tendency to justify other reasons causing our problems, even if it just gives us a glimmer of hope, only to avoid facing the inevitable, no matter how strong of a person you are, we all do it. However, what I could not understand wasn't Dad thinking about grandma's back surgery as he tried to convince himself he needed it? Obviously, it was on my mind.

The doctor ordered more tests to make sure he was going in the right direction. This meant Dad had to stay in the hospital for a couple of days. To us it felt like forever. The doctor really put him through the wringer. He did not leave any stone unturned, as he ordered a myelogram and a CT scan of his spine, we all waited, crossing our fingers, until all his tests came back. I know the waiting was unbearable for him as well.

Here we were, preparing for Dad to have this surgery even if it meant it could be risky, when all of a sudden, the bottom fell out and our hopes vanished. This incident was our first bout with our emotions. It seemed as we went through this journey with Dad's illness, whenever we had some hope to hang on to, it never lasted long, just like riding a roller coaster with our feelings, up and down throughout Dad's ordeal.

I remember being in the room when his tests came back. As the doctor told Dad his results, my heart sank. He proceeded to say, "Mr. Gutherie, I don't think back surgery is necessary. Your test shows signs of a degenerative arthritis but there wasn't any lesion impinging on the spinal cord that would call for surgery." Then he said," we need to send you to a neurologist to do some more tests. There's no reason to stay in the hospital it can be done as an out patient," at least we were relieved he could go home.

This time he ordered an electromyography sensory test, an examination of the spinal fluid and a muscle biopsy. It took a couple of weeks for the results to come back. By then to our shock, Dad was already starting to have trouble with his balance. We could not believe how fast this was happening. He became very cautious with his walking. I think when he fell in the airport it made him feel uneasy. He certainly didn't need any broken bones to complicate things.

I have to say it felt like eternity as we anxiously waited for the phone call for the results. I could not begin to imagine how Dad felt. Mom said every time the phone rang her and Ray would rush to answer it. I am glad I was at home with my children to keep my mind occupied or I would have been running to the phone also.

Finally, the doctor called to give Dad the results as he proceeded to say he wanted him to come to his office so he could discuss it in person. Being as anxious as he was Dad wanted to go right then but office hours over. All that waiting until the next day only brought more tension in the house making it a very long night.

The next morning Dad did not want to drive to the doctor's office. Since he was nervous about his balance, he became leery about driving. It was hard seeing Dad lose his confidence like that. I knew then this was serious for him to feel that way. Mom did not have a driver's license so I volunteered to drive. For some reason mom did not want to go along with us. I could not understand that, I know she was scared but that would not have stopped me. Although, I was relieved I did not have to go alone, my sister-in-law, Karen, came with us. I had a sinking feeling I was going to need moral support and Jim was working. The drive to the doctor's office seemed to be the quietest ride I ever took. I guess we all knew we were facing a serious situation with Dad, but thought if we did not say anything maybe it would not happened

When we got to the doctor's office, I insisted on going into the examining room with Dad while Karen waited. You know how daughters are with their Dads. I wanted to make sure he was going to be okay. Since it was obvious he was having trouble with his balance, I knew he needed help getting on the examining table.

My Dad was a very proud man, he would never ask for any assistance from the doctor or the staff. However, in my opinion I felt the office staff should have noticed I needed help getting Dad to the examining room. After all, they're trained for situations like that. All they did was show us to the room and said," the doctor will be with you shortly." That was my first clue things were not going to turn out very well. Where was the compassion in that office?

Of course, at this point I was hurting and very sensitive to what was happening to my Dad, so maybe I was a little bitter, but that was how I felt. I was certainly glad I was there with him. Nevertheless, when the doctor came in to give Dad his test results for a split second I thought to myself, maybe I would have been better off hearing about this diagnosis second hand and not in person. Even before he said anything, I knew it was going to be bad news.

I will never forget the way the doctor explained to Dad. I cannot even imagine a professional being that cold hearted. There was no compassion in his voice. Not once did the doctor ask Dad if he was okay, or if he was comfortable. He was such a **matter of fact type of a doctor**. In my opinion, he needed to go back to school and learn some type of compassion.

The doctor proceeded to tell Dad about the test results and did not sugar coat a thing, h**e came right out and said, "Mr. Gutherie, after the entire tests were back we found you have a neurological disease." The doctor did not even say I am sorry to tell you this; he did not even blink an eye. He just blurted out "A.L.S., a rapid progressive neurological disease**." I could not believe what he just said. I felt like punching him in the face, that's how mad I was. That was a lot to digest! I certainly did not know what in the hell he meant by A.L.S. I never heard of it before. Although, I knew this doctor was going to tell us and not hold anything back.

As I looked over at Dad, I could tell by the tears in his eyes he knew it was going to be something like this. "Well," Dad said, "I guess we finally have a title to this unknown family illness," then there was silence. It was the second time in my life I saw my Dad's eyes tear up. I stood there with this shocking look on my face, all I heard was the beating of my heart. I just wanted to pretend this was not happening. All I wanted was my Dad to say it is going to be okay but instead it was I doing the comforting. I kept on thinking repeatedly, **WHAT IN THE WORLD WAS THIS DISEASE!** There was no doubt I was in denial this was not happening to my Dad! **I have seen it happen to other people, but not us, in my mind my family was different.**

Trying to get my composure while the shock wore off, I asked the doctor to explain exactly what we were dealing with and "**how can we get help for Dad.**" I was bursting with all kinds of questions that needed answers. I could not stop from talking. It was rapid fire. I was in a panic mode because I never gave the doctor the chance to respond. No one was going to tell me there was nothing we could do for Dad. All I did was ramble on and on. Karen was out in the waiting room and I know she heard my fearful voice.

In my mind I figure if something would keep this disease at this stage, it would be better than doing nothing at all. Dad could still lead a normal life. At least we would be grateful we caught it in time before it did too much damage.

You know the strangest thing about all of this was, here my Dad was letting me ramble on not once did he say, "Pam, settle down, and give the doctor a chance to talk". He just sat there.

As the room became quiet, I took a deep breath trying to take all of this in. Then the nightmare started. As if this was not enough information to digest, he gave us all the negative details about this disease. At that moment all my dreams just vanished into mid air, making me feel like it was the end of the world and there was no hope. I felt like we were falling into a deep hole and there was no getting out. Our life, our normalcy in the family, was gone! No one could ever get it back for us.

The doctor stated, "It would be unfair not to tell you the inevitable about this terrible disease. It's called **Amyotrophic Lateral Sclerosis A.L.S.** better known as **Lou Gehrig's disease,** regrettably, it is an

incurable disease. At this point, there is not even a drug to slow it down. You need to go home and prepare yourself and the family for what lies ahead of you. *"*

Then he proceeded to tell us what to expect with this devastating disease. "You see" he said, "this disease robs your muscles of all movement, to the point it will eventually cause complete paralysis. It does not affect your mind for it remains fully functional, but without muscle function, you will lose everything, even all your means of communication. Many times this has been explained as **A DISEASE THAT MAKES YOU FEEL LIKE A PRISONER TRAPPED IN YOUR OWN BODY."**

I just stood there with my mouth open in a state of disbelief. I could not believe what he just told us, I would have been better off not knowing. When I glanced towards my Dad, I saw this look of helplessness on his face. I didn't know what to do or how to comfort him.

I sometimes wonder if it would have been better for me if I were not with him that day. **Now** I cannot help remembering that look of despair on his face, it will haunt me for the rest of my life. All of a sudden, I had this numbing sensation come over me thinking about how this is such a humbling way for anyone to die, especially our Dad. Here he was "our rock" ending his life this way. I could not imagine how we were going to get through this.

When the doctor finished with his diagnosis, he gave Dad some advice. "Save your strength" he said, "don't go searching for other answers; they will only lead you back to **the same diagnosis—A.L.S."**

Now come on I thought to myself, how he expects us not to seek out a second opinion. The reality was after everything we went through the doctor was right. It did lead us right back to the same diagnosis, **but we had to try!**

When we came out of the room, Karen was waiting in the hall. She did not have to ask a thing she could tell it was terrible news and she was not ready to face it. I know she needed Rick her husband, by her side for comfort before we told her the bad news.

The drive back home felt like forever. Dad could not stop talking about mom. He was very concerned for her and kept on saying repeatedly "I don't know what mom is going to do." It was obvious he was more concerned for her than himself. He did not know how he was going to tell her. He could not stop thinking about her, wondering if she had the strength to get through this.

The reality was mom did have a feeling the bad news was coming. It was not as if she had not seen this before. She was the one that always took care of grandma when she was ill. I know it was always in the back of her mind all her life also. She was aware of all the signs, praying it would never happen to Dad.

The thoughts were racing through my mind as we drove home. The more I thought about what the doctor told us the madder I became. I kept on thinking that doctor was nuts if he thought we were not going to get a second opinion. We are not giving up that easy. Furthermore, doctors are not God; they could very easily make mistakes. Why should we sit back and let this disease take over Dad. Look at how many years he was there for us. We are a family and we will pull together! I could have gone on and on I was so mad at him. I know my face was beet red with anguish.

My Dad was deep in thought also because it was so quiet in the car. Then all of a sudden, he said, "that's it I'm going to get a second opinion." I've heard a lot of great things about the Mayo Clinic and that's where I'm going!" I was so glad he was thinking the same way I was it made it easier telling the rest of the family when we got home. We all needed some hope to hang on too.

You can imagine the chaos in the room when Dad told everyone. Nevertheless, after the panic stopped it was full speed ahead and on to the Mayo Clinic. Our only question was how soon we could get him in. We knew time was not on our side. Dad's body was rapidly deteriorating

We were fully aware that this was not going to be an easy trip for Dad or us. Living in a different state than the Clinic, we knew we would have to fly, but that was not going to stop us. In fact, we were not going to let any hurdles ever again get in our way. This was our

Dad and he needed our help. It was like reverse role-play we were the ones now taking charge.

There was a very long waiting list to get into the Mayo Clinic. You needed an appointment months in advance. We were fortunate Dad's physician was able to pull some strings and get him an appointment within four weeks, which still was a long time if you're only sitting around waiting. We felt it was important to keep Dad's attitude positive as we tried to find a way to occupy his mind.

It was the beginning of spring which living in Michigan it's still very cold and dreary, and waiting around trying to kill time can be depressing especially for someone in Dad's condition. Dad was on sick leave from work so he did not have work to occupy him. That's when we all came up with the idea to go to Florida. There is no better place to keep your mind occupied than the condominium and the beautiful beaches.

He so loved the beach and the warm air. Your mind just floated away in the sunset. Florida has a peaceful serenity about it especially listening to the sounds of the ocean. We all know how fast time flies when your having fun. It would help to keep Dad's mind occupied watching the grandkids having fun. Since it was spring break, the timing was great for us to go. What a perfect place for Dad to regroup his thoughts, at least for a little while.

While we were in Florida, we could not help thinking maybe this would be Dad's last time being here, so we were determined to make it his best. The kids were having a great time. Although, it was starting to become obvious to them Dad was having trouble with his walking. I know they felt something was seriously wrong because us adults hovered over him like hawks, making sure, he never went anywhere alone. We certainty did not want him to fall again. I know he was getting flustered with us; however, we were not letting him out of our sight.

His walking was becoming uncertain and we did not need any complications with a fall. We insisted on Dad using crutches to help him with his balance. Of course, being stubborn and proud he felt there was no need for it yet. He quickly changed his mind after an incident one night when we all went out to dinner. Dad was getting ready to open the car door when all of a sudden he lost his balance and almost fell trying to get in the car. If Rick and Jim had not caught him, his legs would have ended up under the car and who knows; maybe he would have had two broken legs to deal with. I know that really scared him. It was the first time Dad felt he wasn't invincible. That in itself was a very humbling feeling for him.

When the grandkids saw what happened to grandpa they became very quiet and upset. There certainly were many questions that night about Dad. Trying to reassure them everything was going to be alright was hard, especially when they could see for themselves the changes in Dad's health. By the look on our faces, they could tell we were not sure either.

At this point not even the doctors could tell us what to expect with this disease. Yes, they knew the outcome, and did not hold anything back telling us that, but no one could predict how it was going to progress, or what part of his body was going to feel the affect first. We were on our own.

One thing we knew for sure was we had to hide our feelings from the kids for a little while longer, at least until we had a second opinion about Dad's health from the Mayo Clinic, which we were praying would change his diagnosis.

Spring break was over and the kids needed to be back to school so we left Florida and headed back to Michigan. It was hard for us to leave Dad in Florida since he had three more weeks to go before he came home, but with Ray staying with mom and Dad made us feel comfortable.

By this time, he needed to use a walker to get around. It was sad to see how he went from using crutches to this walker; it only reinforced the reality how quickly Dad was losing the ability to walk.

When Dad came home, I cannot tell you the shock it was when we saw Ray pushing him in a wheelchair. I could not believe my eyes. We knew his legs were getting weaker, but that was fast! Within a matter of three weeks, he went from walking, to needing help from crutches, now a wheelchair! His whole deterioration with his legs took only five weeks to do its damage. That is how rapid this disease was progressing. If we did not witness it with our own eyes, we would have never believed it. **Where was the justice?**

CHAPTER 14

The Mayo Clinic confirmed the devastated diagnosis

Dad's health was changing so fast that when he received the phone call to come to the Mayo Clinic for his appointment we were relieved hoping it was not too late to help him. Of course, also hoping maybe this wasn't A.L.S.

Our next step was to determine who was going with them to help with Dad. Everyone wanted to be a part of being there. Although since we had to fly mom couldn't possibly take everyone. We still had to be practical with the expense. Mom knew she needed two of my brothers to go especially with the lifting of Dad. She asked Rick and Ray. For myself, I could not imagine staying home and waiting for updates on Dad that would have driven me nuts. Since I was the oldest mom chose me also. I guess age had its privileges.

The reality was I was the only one that did not have little ones. My children were older and in middle school at that time, so it was much easier for me to get away. It was important to them that Karen, Rick's wife went also; she always helped them in the past with all their insurance papers. Always making sure everything was documented and ready to file. She was like their private secretary. In addition; she was a good listener and never assumed anything or jumped the gun. We always had a tendency to do that. Karen and Rick did have a little one at home, although he was not in school yet so it was easier leaving him with a relative.

I don't know what Dad would have done if he didn't have Ray, he really depended on Ray for most of his lifting. He was the youngest and strongest. I think that is when Ray acquired the nickname from Dad (the mule). Ray definitely lived up to it. He was such a big help for Dad. He helped to take a lot of the burden off mom's shoulders. Thank God, he was still living at home. The family was very fortunate Ray decided not to move. I know it was fate.

When we drove down to the airport that morning just thinking about how we were going to get Dad on the plane, made us nervous not knowing what to expect. Nevertheless, it did spark Ray's sense of humor telling jokes about all the ways we could get Dad on the airplane. When he started pantomiming all the ways, he got everyone laughing their head off, especially Dad. He said, "you know we can put Dad on a blanket and drag him down the aisle." He went on and on all the way to the airport. One thing we did find out was how prepared the Airlines are to handle situations like Dad's. If we had known ahead of time, we would have had one less thing to worry about. At least the laughter broke up the tension with Ray's jokes.

When we arrived at the Mayo Clinic and checked Dad in, we found the hotel next door had an adjoining tunnel to the clinic and we never had to go outside. While Dad was going through his tests, walking back and forth through the tunnel helped to work off our tension. It gave us a feeling we were staying right with him. The best part of all this, was as long as he wasn't scheduled to have any tests that day we could take him back and forth with us.

The doctors were very thorough with everything they did to him; they even re-did the tests he had before just to make sure. We knew if any hospital could find answers to Dad's illness, it was here.

Finding things to kill time was not difficult with this group; we were always looking for ways to entertain ourselves since we were there for a week. One good thing about my family was our sense of humor. When we were together, we were always laughing and telling jokes. We could amuse ourselves all day long with that. In a way with all our own lives being busy at home it was nice to share that closeness again, a bonding I truly missed.

I remember one joke the boys played on Dad. Since they allowed us to take Dad back and forth from the hospital we thought, it would be a nice break for him to have restaurant food for a change. You know how everyone really loves the taste of hospital food. Although we had to make sure, he was back in his room before visiting hours were over. For once, we had the upper hand; we really milked it to the fullest. Teasing Dad and letting him know he was in our power and if he did not behave he was going right back to his room to have hospital food for dinner.

We all joked about how good it felt to give Dad some rules for a change. Imagine telling the man who we all feared when we were kids, especially when we heard those scary words come out of mom's mouth, "wait until your father comes home". We could not wait to give it back to him, "you better behave or you're going to have to eat hospital food." Dad certainly got a big kick out of our humor after all we inherited it from him.

The next day, my two brothers still looking for ways to amuse themselves, had mom in a wheelchair alongside Dad's and ran down the tunnel pushing them for a race. The girls kept on yelling at them to be careful; even though we knew, mom and Dad were not in any danger. It's funny, as long as the thought no one was watching them they would have fun. However, if they remembered about the security cameras in the tunnel they would have died with embarrassment knowing someone really was watching them.

The things we did to amuse ourselves never surprised mom she was used to it and always went with the flow. An old proverb said, "laughter is the best medicine." I agree with that because it made us forget why we were there at least for a little while. If we could not find a way to kill time the waiting would have been unbearable.

I will never forget all the ups and downs we went through with our emotions while we were there. Every time a new test came back, the doctors were confused about Dads diagnosis again. Making remarks referring to his symptoms as not proof enough to say it was A.L.S. These doctors were the cream of the crop, and when they were puzzled, it made you feel like maybe there was hope, especially when the last doctor gave him the diagnosis of A.L.S. without even blinking an eye.

I have heard stories with people misdiagnosed. This could easily happen to us as we hung on to a glimmer of hope. We even started to believe we finally were getting Dad some help. In our thinking, if the doctors found a way to stop the progression of this disease, we could still handle Dad's handicap the way he is now and be grateful. Dad not being able to walk was no big deal to us, especially thinking about his alternative. Perhaps even thinking he may even have a different neurological disorder they could cure. All of those thoughts were going through our minds; we even had Dad believing that. The bottom line was, whatever his diagnosis was we would try to do our best to handle it.

I did notice how cautious these doctors were with giving us any information about Dad's diagnosis. They kept on referring to his symptoms as not a **textbook case of A.L.S.** To us the Mayo Clinic was the word of God whatever they said we were ready to accept, our searching finish. As other tests came back repeatedly, the doctors kept telling us something does not make any sense. To me that meant they were not giving up until they ruled out everything. That is when I felt confident we were in the right place for our Dad.

CHAPTER 15

The Morning the bomb dropped causing a panic as we digest Dad's future care

Then one morning after all of Dad's tests were finished, Karen, Rick, Ray, and I were asked to come to a meeting at the Genetics Doctors' office. It was right before Dad was released from the hospital. The doctor was insisting that everyone come except mom and Dad. We could not figure out why he was only concerned with just us, after all they were involved too. I tried to make light of the situation, telling my family he probably wanted to make sure we were emotionally ready to handle Dad's illness without them being there. Trying hard to reassure myself, I was right. Still hoping as I expressed my feelings to my family that maybe he is even going to give us a different diagnosis.

Then for a split second, I started to wonder why was a genetic doctor talking to us about Dad's diagnosis? Something definitely wasn't adding up. Shouldn't this talk be coming from his neurologist? However, I did not want to cause a panic and scare everyone by telling them my feelings. I just crossed my fingers and hoped for the best.

Words could not express what happened to us in that office. Absolutely no one could have prepared us for this! What the doctor revealed to us that day put us all into shock, as if a huge rock just struck us and nothing could stop the bleeding. This is when our world came tumbling down.

As he started talking he said, "all the tests show your father definitely has A.L.S." With a confusing look on our faces, he could tell we had a hard time understanding that comment. The last we heard the doctors were still speculating on his symptoms not fitting the so-called textbook case of A.L.S. So how do we digest that news? Looking at the expression on our faces, he tried to explain it further. You see, he said Familial A.L.S. is the hereditary form of this disease. With this type, symptoms can be completely different with each patient, ruling out the "textbook cases". Still not, deriving a conclusion, that now this was going to affect us; we just sat there waiting until he finished talking about Dad's illness. The room became very quiet as we all tried to digest everything we just heard.

Then he dropped the **BOMB.** "Your father told me maybe there was something like this in your family with your grandmother." We just sat there looking surprised waiting to here what he was going to say next. This was the first time we heard Dad had these concerns.

I know Dad told us about his fears that Sunday in his kitchen, thinking that he might be coming down with the same illness grandma had. However, never did we think it might be a hereditary illness. The only thing I remember him saying was he might be ill. I completely blocked out everything else. I was too concerned for his health to hear anymore. Anyway, heredity was the furthest thing from Dad's mind, so we thought. He never let on to us as we were growing up that there was ever any history of a family hereditary disorder.

Now I understood why we were at the Genetics Doctor office. I was so scared I was hoping no one read it on my face. As the doctor went on to say, "if the speculations of the family having this history are true, although we have no records to authentic it, then your father's diagnosis becomes Familial A.L.S., which means it is **inherited** and will be passed on." As I sat there listening my heart sank into my shoes.

Then I realized why mom and Dad were not in the doctor's office with us that day. I know now they could not take seeing us get the news in which all those years they were hoping would never surface. It was too hard for them to face us.

Then the doctor tried to explain to as cautiously as he could. **"Unfortunately hereditary means that every sibling has a fifty**

percent chance of getting this disease. This is a very rare type of A.L.S. he said, which was the reason your Dad's diagnosis was so complicated. Only five percent of the cases who come down with A.L.S. will find it to be hereditary. Sadly you will still never know for sure until another family member becomes ill, which we pray that never happens."

My advice to the family is to go on with your lives and try to block this out because right now your Dad needs all of your help. I know mentally this will be hard for the family to do, but it is important for your entire wellbeing to feel this will never happen. You cannot live the rest of your lives in fear. That will be more damaging than waiting for the disease to strike."

As I looked around the room to see the expressions on my siblings' faces, I will never forget the look on Rays. He did not say one word he just got up as if he was in a trance and left the room. I remember thinking we are going home soon and he needs to be with us, where is he going. I wanted to run after him and tell him it is going to be okay but I did not believe it either. At that moment, I could not support anyone. I was feeling the same way, as if my world, my life, was over. My mind was going out of control thinking if this doctor made the right decision giving us this scenario; after all, we still had no proof. Now here we are back to the beginning again facing the unknown. Why couldn't he just let us concentrate on Dad and not worry about the "what-ifs?"

If it was not for my husband and my two daughters at home, I do not know what I would have done. Here we were raising children of our own now it was our turn to carry this devastating secret.

My first reaction was to give up right then. I remember saying to Rick, "maybe it would be easier if I get this nightmare over right now and walk right out in the road in front of a car." Wondering to myself how did Dad stay so strong to carry this burden all those years? I knew I had to find the same strength.

When I came to my senses and settled down, I realized for the first time in my life I was not the type to give up. Never to have been challenged before, I didn't know it was in me. I had to be strong for my own family when I got home. My life had to carry on no matter what was ahead.

At that moment I made a decision to myself I was going to focus only on the words the doctors said," until it was proven to be hereditary." Hoping and praying no one else in the family would ever come down with this terrible disease.

It was important to me to make sure this did not affect my girls. They were teenagers now and had the right to a normal life. They were suffering enough watching grandpa slowly die, which was hard for any of us let alone the kids. It would not be fair to them to carry this burden. We all have fond memories of being teenagers and they deserved theirs.

My oldest Daughter, Kim, was graduating from high school and Kristie was just starting. They were old enough to understand that we were trying hard not to show our fears. Trying to reassure them at the time, we were not giving up on grandpa. We are going to get through this and find a way to help him.

For now, I felt there was no need to let them know about the hereditary aspect. If this curse happens again then that would be the time to let them know. I was not about to ruin their young lives. As I thought about this decision, I now know how Dad felt not letting us know about this potential family health crisis. Now, I was doing the same thing. Still hanging on to the hope we still had no proof this was hereditary, furthermore we didn't want any.

This disease was still puzzling to us. We still did not have any answers. Not knowing much about it made us more aggressive to research anything we could find that could help Dad. We were not going to leave any stone unturned. **Even though I did say we were going to accept the Mayo Clinic diagnosis and quit searching for other alternatives,—the reality was I LIED!** We were never giving up. Our hope and our determination became the fuel that kept us going.

However, telling the rest of the family about this awful news when we got home was going to be impossible. As thoughts raced through my mind, I was worried mostly for Ray, Ron, and Sue, with this news.

They had no loving companion to help give them support besides the family; we all needed the extra comfort now.

Still in the doctor's office trying hard to digest all of this, Rick decided he needed to change the mood in the room. Out came the comical storyteller in him **again**. He thought if he could get us all talking about the old days and reminisce about our childhood it may bring out some laughter, which we certainly needed right now. He tried very hard to find a way to cheer us up. Normally he was very good at that, this time I was not in a mood to listen. Of course, that did not stop Rick. He was determined to talk your ear off with the stories. I have to admit sometimes as a brother he was a nuisance but he was always entertaining.

Dad was the one who always got the biggest kick from Rick. He knew his stories were fabricated, but it never stopped Dad from laughing until his eyes were all teary. When Rick was in the room, you always knew it by the roar of laughter. It was funny how Rick acquired the title the Storyteller in the family. It stayed with him all his life. His mind was like reading a book. At every family gathering he loved being the center of attention, which he milked for all its worth. Rick was always the first to start talking and the last to stop. If he were asked to speak in front of an audience, he would have never hesitated. Later on in his life, that is where his career ended up. Rick became a Motivational Speaker for Ford Motor Company standing up in front of his co-workers talking up a storm. There was no doubt he found his niche in life. He truly loved it. In fact being in front of an audience gave him the incentive to be great at it. As he finished talking about the good old days our childhood and the fun we had growing up, since we could not get him to shut up, he **did make us feel better,—at least for a little while.**

When we left the doctors office, we went back to Dad's room to check him out of the hospital. As we tried to think of ways to break this news to the rest of the family when we got home we notice Ray was not with us. Slowly walking into Dad's room not knowing what to expect we saw mom and Dad nervously waiting for us. All of a sudden, we ran into their arms and found ourselves sharing a group hug. Just standing there shaking with fear, not wanting to ever let go. No words spoken; no tears shed; only hugs shared. Dad had this panic look on his face when he realized Ray was not with us, knowing that Ray would have been the one to take this news the worst.

When Dad's voice started to tremble asking, "where is Ray"? I felt terrible telling him how Ray reacted in the doctor's office. It was hard for Dad to hold back his tears. Then the room became very quiet as you could see this concerned look on Dad's face for Ray. "Dad" I said, "don't worry he will be waiting for us outside, he knows we're going home."

The nurse came in the room with the wheelchair to escort Dad out of the hospital when his doctor insisted he wanted to do it. As he pushed Dad's wheelchair to the commuter car waiting to take us to the airport, there stood Ray. He was standing in the cold holding on to his suitcase looking like it was the end of the world. Ray knew he needed time to himself fully knowing we would be there soon. Gingerly the doctor helped Dad into the car. I remember him saying while shaking Dad's hand, "Mr. Gutherie I just wish I was sending you home to the rest of your family with good news. If there is ever anything I can do for you please don't hesitate to call me." You know, this was the first time no one told jokes on the way home. In fact, no one spoke; not even Rick, he was lost for words. Brining this news home as we told the rest of the family of the possibility of this disease being hereditary was obvious how it would affect each of us differently.

Rick was convincing himself he was retiring at the age of 50. Not because of being tired of working but from **FEAR**. Fear of thinking if he waited until Dad's age to retire, which was 58, he may not ever have a chance to enjoy it. Sadly, Rick died the year he turned 58 from A.L.S. I know the fear of the unknown with this devastating disease was too much for any of us to bear, especially Rick. Always being on guard thinking okay who was going to be next. He became possessed and was determined to live the rest of his life to the fullest. He could never get the fear out of his mind that he might be a carrier of this terrible gene, especially when he started to have unusual muscle twitching which are the first signs of A.L.S.

Even though the doctor had no proof it was Familial A.L.S., they were obligated to give us the "what-if" scenario, it was their responsibility, as I tried to convince myself of that. Although just hearing that one statement from the doctor was enough to haunt all of us for the rest of our lives.

For Ray, I am not sure at what point this started to happen but he slowly withdrew from the family. Maybe the reason was the thought of losing Dad. You could see him starting to retreat into himself. Ray was always the center of attention when it came to the grandkids. They truly loved and enjoyed him especially his shenanigans, which they still talk about today. He would always instigate many ideas for the grandkids to do, fully knowing they would get into trouble, and then when grandma yelled at them, Ray would take off running so it did not look like he was the one that caused it. The family Sunday dinners he enjoyed as much as Dad did, which was sad to give up. At least it got us all together once a week.

However, he did become closer to Sue and Mary, my younger sisters, and became more of a buddy to Brother Ron. They were the four youngest siblings growing up together, which made their bond stronger. At least I was happy to see him not withdraw from the family totally.

Don't get the wrong idea, we knew Ray loved us all and the feeling was mutual, after all he was our little brother. Nevertheless, the fun we all had being together was no more. Our family and our lives were changing rapidly. It was hard losing that worry free attitude "life is a bed of roses." Reality was setting in.

Sister Sue, who was the second youngest in the family, had a terrible time with this news. Before all of this happened she was going through some life changes of her own, which only added to her crisis. It was hard for her to see Dad slowly deteriorating. Unfortunately, her release became drinking and drugs which totally got out of control. After Dad's death, she started to get her life back on track. I know he would have been very proud of her.

As for me the closer, I became to Dad's age, the more I too was possessed with fear. I would not have been able to maintain my emotions as I went through my ups and downs, had it not been for my loving husband and two daughters. I always tried to focus on Dad's illness and not on the "what-ifs."

It was different with mom; she knew what was ahead. She was there when grandma died with the same illness. Yes, we had a tremendous challenge ahead. Yes, the road was really going to get bumpy along this journey. However, to give up was not in our nature. We realized we inherited a valuable characteristic from Dad, which became obvious as we continued with his care. It was his strength, endurance, and determination, which became the fuel that kept us going.

Taking this news hard only made us stronger to face the challenge to help with Dad's care. Sister Linda, who was the youngest of the oldest four siblings, 32 at that time, was the one mostly in denial with Dad's illness. This became a good thing for the family. She was determined not to take the *no hope* as a verdict for his diagnosis. Her attitude became contagious to the rest of us, which started a ripple effect.

Linda and I were the closest among the girls, there was no way I was going to let her do this alone. Our emotions became contagious with the rest of the family, in no time at all everyone came on board. This endeavor became easy; at least for us, both our husbands supported our efforts all the way. There was never any pressure of being gone all the time, which caring for Dad did consumed a lot.

In the beginning, none of us complained. Most of the time it was Linda, Mary and Karen, and I, and of course brother Ray dug in. As we adjusted, it became part of our normal routine. We could not imagine not being there to help Dad; after all, he was there for us for many years. Now, it was our turn to be there for him.

Soon everyone in the family started taking on chores of anything and everything that made mom and Dad's life easier. Karen, my sister-in-law retained the role of being mom's private secretary, along with helping with Dad. She always made sure her bills were always in order; mom had enough on her mind with Dad's care. Paula, Bob's wife, would come and help with laundry and yard work when she could.

Even though mom always had us girls around, Ray being there 24 hours a day, especially to help with the lifting of Dad, was a relief for mom's wellbeing. The rest of the brothers were working so they did what they could. Just being company for Dad and telling him how their day went was great therapy for him. It was funny though, after all those years of growing up and not being able to tell Dad about their day because he was always to busy with his work, now they finally had his total attention.

There is no doubt with Mary being around a lot was a huge help for mom. Even before Dad became ill, Mary loved helping around their house, at the same time earning pocket some money. It was mom's way of helping her out.

When little Renée, Mary's daughter tagged along it was a joy for both mom and Dad. She could keep herself entertained all day long while Mary clean the house and helped with Dad at the same time. Everyone knew that she was grandma's little girl but she enjoyed Dad's company too.

However, I have to say when Karen and Rick brought their little Kyle over their son; he always managed to steel Dad's heart. He was so much like his Dad, Rick, which Dad got a big kick out of seeing. Dad enjoyed watching Kyle putting on a show for him with his learning abilities. We always referred to Kyle as Rick and Karen's little puppet. They always had him performing in front of us. There was no doubt, where Kyle got his showmanship. With only being two years old Dad was amazed how he could count to ten in German and how good he was reciting and recognizing the alphabet. He certainly was entertainment for Dad.

With all of us helping in many different ways only firmed up how strong our family bond was. At this point in Dad's illness having Ray and mom around while we were at our own homes worked out fine for all of us, it's amazing how we all became great jugglers. I remember a comment Dad once said to mom about with a big smile on his face, "**now** I know why we had eight kids."

CHAPTER 16

Dad's positive attitude even with sick leave

Throughout all of this, I could not believe how remarkable Dad's morale and spirit was. I cannot say it enough. There's no doubt our strength came from him. Each phase Dad went through with this disease he never became depressed and always remained positive. What a roll model he was for us. Dad had the ability to turn a negative situation into a positive one, always making light of the things he could still do. He always took his illness one day at a time.

I fondly remember one remark he made about being in a wheelchair. "So what if I can't walk anymore, I'm still a very lucky man. I can still use my arms and my hands making me still feel independent, and I can be grateful I can still breath on my own, that I know is a blessing."

It was strange; at times Dad looked like he was reassuring us. Even with his doom and gloom diagnosis, making this remark, "I've been told miracles do happen." Now that really threw me off guard. Religion was never big on his list. As he finished he said," if God wanted to be on my side he would be very grateful for his help." Can you imagine that type of attitude after getting this diagnosis from the infallible Mayo Clinic? **Now that is a positive attitude!**

Dad's life certainly had a lot of adjusting to do especially with work, which was the hardest for him. Even though he was on temporary sick leave from Ford Motor Company, they still provided a way for him to stay busy working at home. It was great therapy for Dad; it made him feel as if he was still in the loop of things. At least for a little while it helped to keep his mind occupied.

It was amazing when the word got out about Dad's illness. Hearing the concerns of everyone and all their stories about how much respect there was for Dad in the industry was overwhelming. A side of Dad we never realized. We always knew he loved his work. For him to climb the ladder as he did, proved to me he must have done a good job. However, for his co-workers to make that comment truly made you feel proud. I know we would not have known that side of him if it were not for his illness.

It seemed like everyone was worried and praying for him, especially his friends and co-workers who interacted with him on a daily basis. Not to see Dad at work was unusual for them, they knew something had to be serious with his health. Even his old high school friends contact him when they heard the news. Everyone made a point of calling or sending cards. He truly was respected among his peers, and fondly appreciated among his friends. It is no wonder we had visitors coming by the house all the time. He even saw his staff often for meetings. I know they could have kept in contact by phone or computer, but they wanted to see Dad in person. It certainly lifted his spirit.

Their house seemed to have had a revolving door. Even though at this point in his illness Dad's legs were the only thing affected with this disease, he was still capable of having somewhat of a normal life style, and was not embarrassed to have visitors, for now everyone was comfortable being around him. For awhile, it was great, it gave you a feeling nothing had changed with him.

CHAPTER 17
A special day the Taurus and Sable

Oh, how I remember this special day. Mom received a phone call from Dad's head engineer asking her if Dad was up to having a special treat. He explained to mom that 30 members of his staff, along with the two prototype cars, the Taurus and Sable, would like to come out to the house for a surprise visit. Making sure, it would be okay with her. With excitement in her voice as she almost lost it over the phone trying to hold back the tears, said that would be wonderful, Al will be thrilled.

Well when she told all of us, the excitement in the house was overwhelming. Dad knew something was up when all of us kids showed up at the house all at once. It was hard for us not to ruin the surprise especially when we kept going back and forth outside to check on their arrival.

It was amazing to watch this procession of cars come down the street; it felt like Dad was a movie star. When we took Dad outside to watch them, pull into the driveway the look he had on his face was priceless. We certainly needed many tissues right at that moment.

None of this was possible if it wasn't for one person whom I personal want to thank, Clancy, who was manager of the Forward Model Luxury and Large Car Chassis & Power train Design Engineering Department, Luxury & Large Car Engineering & Planning at that time. To me it was remarkable how he coordinated all of this, especially with these cars, which were not in the dealerships yet. I always wondered how his group pulled that off. What you did for our Dad, words can never express enough!

Man, did heads turn when they came down the street. Neighbors were coming out of their houses to see what was going on. What a beautiful day it became. Earlier in the morning, it was raining and we were worried about having Dad outside in the wheelchair; thank goodness, the rain had stopped.

Seeing Dad get choked up as he examined these cars was hard to take. Typical engineer you could feel him wishing he could have gotten out of the wheelchair to get in the driver's seat. I know it was eating him up inside. It was a very emotional day for all of us as we watched his eyes light up like a proud Dad who saw his babies for the first time. In a way, that's what it was, a birth of twins. Dad took his time looking them all over, even looking under the hood at the engine, as if he was giving them his final inspection for his stamp of approval.

The pictures we took of that day were priceless. Now when his great grandkids and their kids see the pictures it will tell the story about what their great grandpa not only did for a living, but how well.

After seeing Dad, interacting with everyone that day made me feel like his health was actually stabilizing and he was going into remission. I know I was only dreaming but just for a split second, I thought maybe God was giving us a sign that Dad was going to be okay. Figuring he had suffered enough and it was time to put a halt to his progression. Unfortunately, it became the total opposite. At least we all had that day to cherish.

CHAPTER 18

Pulling together—finding professional help—adjusting to changes—while cherishing the funny episodes along the way

We were not prepared with how fast Dad's health was deteriorating. We finally reached the point of not knowing which way to turn, let alone what to do next. There were no road maps to follow with this disease. At least one that we were interested in, we were on our own.

Yes, we had the doctors at the Mayo Clinic whenever needed but we could not keep going back whenever he had a problem it was too far away. Naturally, we were not going back to the first doctor, you know the one without the compassion.

That is when we decided it was time to be our own health advocates. We frantically researched doctors that were familiar with neuromuscular disorders mainly A.L.S. To us it was important especially if we ever had a crisis with Dad, at least we would not be wasting any valuable time going from one doctor to another.

Feverishly Linda began the quest to find a doctor that could not only help in Dad's care, but who could also be open minded to other types of alternative health treatment. We realized the medical field didn't have much knowledge on this disease especially the Familial A.L.S. At this point in Dad's illness, we felt we had nothing to lose.

Even though we were all busy searching for Professional help, having Dad home all the time was something we weren't use to, for the first time we finally had his total attention. Even thought his illness caused him to be home, we took advantaged of it and enjoyed his company to the fullest.

When we were growing up, he was always working long hours. Therefore, when he finally got home he was too tired to give us his full attention. As little kids we all desired that from him, but we understood and managed to get used to it. I think that was why I enjoyed seeing Dad give his undivided attention to the grandkids; despite the fact, his illness was responsible for slowing him down. It was cute how Dad became their captive audience. It never bothered the little ones seeing Dad in a wheelchair, although the older grandkids knew the healthier side of him before his illness, now seeing him this way was hard for them to come to terms with.

Mom's life had a lot of adjusting to do also. Even though she was not the one that was sick, her life as she once knew came to a complete halt. Mom spent most of her time tending to Dad's needs. At this phase in his illness, she did a lot of waiting on him and helping him with his personal needs. As she put her needs on the back burner for awhile. There wasn't any time for her normal routine, which was something she enjoyed. Mom could spend her whole day doing things around the house and never complain about being bored.

As we all stepped in organizing our time to help keep some of the stress away from mom, it certainly made Dad happy knowing we were taking care of her too. They both knew further down the road what was in store for them was inevitable. Slowly we found out how hard it was to keep this household stress free 24 hours a day.

Dad's care up until now was easy. When we talk about other types of alternative care for Dad, there was one we never wanted to mention; "nursing home," that word was not in our vocabulary at least not yet. Therefore, our main priority was setting up a schedule that would work for all of us.

As we set up this schedule with his care it wasn't all stressful, we did run across a lot of enjoyment as we cherished the many funny moments along the way. We were always trying to make jokes out of every predicament we fell into while caring for Dad. Since his care for now was not life threatening, it made it easy to go with the flow.

I have to tell you though, if you did not have some type of humor with all of this, it would have been very depressing trying to get through. I have said before a sense of humor in the Gutherie family was something none of us lacked, **thank goodness.**

Just for one moment put yourselves into our shoes, how could you have gotten through the day if you could not find a way to make light of Dad's situation. What other choice did we have? Sitting around being depressed was not the way to go. It certainly didn't change the outcome so we had to find some other type of outlet to relieve the stress. For now, it was laughter.

This all started as we realized Dad was struggling to keep up his morning routine by himself. Barely a month went by after he lost the ability to move his legs, when his arms and hands became weaker. Now simple things like putting on a shirt, or being able to brush his hair, or grip a spoon to eat, was becoming harder for him to do on his own. Not having any muscle strength in his arms and hands made it impossible to lift or hold anything. That is how fast his disease was progressing.

We had to step up and face the fact Dad needed our help even more now, especially with his daily needs. As we attempted to prepare for Dad's next phase with his illness, it was obvious there were going to be many adjustments along the way. Since we had no idea what was in store for us we approached it without any fears and proceeded full steam ahead. Never realizing how many embarrassing predicaments were in store for us, or Dad, while caring for him.

For instance, Dad's modesty no longer existed. He had to get used to having his daughters help with personal needs. At times, it must have been a humbling experience for him and no doubt embarrassing for us, but it was something we all had to get over. He was helpless and we had to keep focusing in that direction.

As we organized Dad's daily necessities, we were amazed how many times we ran into different episodes that we never expected to happen. Thankfully, these always turned out to be funny episodes and not serious ones.

I can still picture these two episodes so clearly in my mind that I felt I was there watching it happened all over again. I still get a good laugh from it today.

I remember this one morning, as we got ready to help Dad take a shower. Of course, never did we think we would ever had to be in this position, nevertheless, here we were. In Dad's healthier days, mornings were his favorite times, especially having the feeling of a warm shower to start your day. Now he needed help not only getting in the shower, but also showering him, which at times became very awkward for him and us. With his balance starting to become an issue as long as he could support himself in a sitting position, made it easier for us to help with his shower. Although we still had to be his hands, arms and legs, but that did not bother Dad or us. For now, we were grateful he still had some healthy muscles in his back to help us put our plan to work.

You see with the disease controlling all your muscles even your equilibrium eventually is affected. When the muscles in his back get weaker and die, Dad will no longer be able to support himself as he sits. If he was sitting in a chair and you were not monitoring him he easily could tip over and fall causing complications to his body, like broken bones. Any type of an accident could put Dad in the hospital exposing him to all types of germs; we tried hard to avoid that. We did not need to weaken his immune system anymore than it already was from attacks of infections. However, that worry was down the road no need to be concerned yet, so we carried on with our plan.

As a team we girls started to prepare Dad for his shower, figuring you did not have to be a "rocket scientist" to know how to help him, as we patted ourselves on the back with all kinds of confidence, fully feeling this was going to be a piece of cake knowing we could accomplish anything.

All of a sudden, as we looked at Dad sitting in his wheelchair wondering how we were going to do this, we started to give this idea a second thought. Maybe we may have jumped the gun a bit. This might be a little awkward for us girls to accomplish. Looking towards Ray with this expression of helplessness on our faces, we hurriedly decided to have a better plan by nominating Ray for the job. All he said with this big smile on his face, "I knew you guys would come to that conclusion sooner or later. I will do it only if you girls stay around in case I need your help". Shaking our heads yes **excitedly,** with this look of relief on our faces, we reassured him, "no problem."

Dad started laughing immediately at us girls as we hurriedly shifted the responsibility to Ray, as he made a remark at the same time, "good negotiating skills girls."

Ray started to make his plan on what his part was going to be with the shower scene, as if he was drawing a map "so to speak," going over it again and again in his mind as he told us "you know you can't be too careful, you have to have a plan before you get started." Dad still sitting in his wheelchair waiting to have his shower chuckling to himself saying, "just let me know when you're ready Ray." Thank goodness, Dad wasn't undressed yet he probably would have frozen while waiting for Ray to develop his plan. Finally, Ray said, "ok I think I'm ready." As he looked over towards mom he said, "Now mom, where are you going to be in the bathroom? I want to make sure you're not in my way."

It was amusing how Dad's morning shower turned out to be this big production; something we figured would have been a piece of cake. I have to admit, if it were not for the way Ray handled this episode it would not have been half as funny.

Isn't it amazing how we have a tendency to take everyday necessities for granted until something happens to you? Simple things like taking a shower, how hard could that be? However if you could not stand up anymore or move your hands or arms to wash yourself, then what do you do? In addition, time wise, maybe at the most you are in and out of the shower within 20 minutes, now being incapable of doing it yourself may take an hour, only if you are lucky to have the help. It certainly makes you count your blessings, doesn't it? Dad's shower now took us at least an hour; and half of the time was just getting him prepared to get in.

When I think about people making a career of taking care of patients in their home and how much they go through, I kind of chuckle to myself thinking about us. We now had on- the- job training and we did not have to go to school to earn a degree. The only difference was we were earning **gratitude,** not wages.

We were fortunate to have many pieces of equipment to help care for Dad. A special chair we used for the shower for someone in Dad's condition to sit on made it convenient for him to take a shower. The transfer board we had was awesome. We used it to slide Dad from point A to point B, as it helped to relieve the pressure from pulling on his body and helping us at the same time by saving our backs.

Even with Dad, weighing about two hundred pounds using a lifting belt around his waist, to help move him made Dad feel like he was as light as a feather. I was amazed how smoothly the job went and the best part was Dad wasn't uncomfortable; at least we had all his equipment down pat.

Although with the little grandkids and their great imaginations, they had better ideas for some of Dad's equipment. It did not take them long to turn the transfer board into a slide as they hung it off the couch to slide to the floor, Dad always got a big kick out of watching that.

Ah, but our most efficient piece of equipment was our Ray. You could not put a price on him. He was our most valuable commodity, our lifter. He was always there to move Dad from one area to another. We were thankful Ray put his future on hold to be at home with mom and Dad, providing the assistance they needed.

Finally, as Ray's plan started to unfold, he wheeled Dad into the bathroom and positioned him along side of the tub making sure he was in line with the shower chair.

The rest of us were getting a big kick out of Ray with his so-called plan, as he thought he was so smart. He could not stop boasting and rubbing it in that he did not have to take any special classes, since the family was so adamant about taken care of Dad ourselves at home, the professional suggested we take these classes, however, like Ray said, he didn't need them. As we took these classes, they couldn't stress enough about the importance of proper lifting so no one would throw his or her back out.

Therefore, as we smiled at Ray we said, "if you think your so smart lets see what you can do." He just smiled back and said, "watch the expert do his job." In his mind he had, it all worked out. Only one thing he forgot was how embarrassed he gets when other people's body parts exposed. Never giving it any thought Dad would have to have his private parts exposed, *naturally,* he was going to take a shower.

Ray always was sensitive with those feelings. Even when one of the grandkids were having their diaper changed and he happened to come into the room, he would hurriedly make an about face and walk right out the room with embarrassment all over his face. Of course, that part came easy to the rest of us since we all had families of our own, you get used to exposed body parts now and then, little toddlers love running around the house in their birthday suits.

When Ray was ready to go, we girls decided to sit back and see how long it would take for him to realize he was in store for an embarrassing moment, at the same time laughing to ourselves because we already knew.

He was so cute though, before he got started he left the room and went into his bedroom for a few minutes. Everyone started yelling at him "now where do you think you're going?" Out of the bedroom he came, wearing his bathing suit. As he stood there with this shitty grin on his face looking proud because he had this cool idea all by himself, making a comment to us, "pretty smart don't you think!" When we questioned, "why in the world do you have your bathing suit on?" His comment was, still with this smirk expression on his face, "do I have to spell it out for you? How can I get Dad all wet if I do not climb in the shower with him? This way if I get wet it won't matter because I will have my bathing suit on. We just looked at each other laughing and **had** to admit to Ray "yep you got us, we would have never thought of that." Dad just looked at him with this big grin on his face and said, "Ray, are you finally ready now," as he waited patiently next to the shower.

"Okay," he said to mom," "lets do this" rubbing his hands together. As mom reached over to close the door so Dad would not get cold when he got undressed, we hurriedly ran up to the door to listen. Fully knowing what was going to happen next with Ray as we tried hard to muffle our laughs so he wouldn't get mad at us. Then we heard mom say to Ray, "okay Ray, you get on that side of Dad and when I unbuckle his pants you can pull them off."

All of a sudden it was like a light bulb going off in Ray's head, "wait a minute, he yelled loudly, that's not part of my plan, that's where I won't cross the line, I'm not going to get Dad undressed, that's your job mom, you're his wife and you're used to seeing Dad undressed." As he flew out the door, we had to rush to the other room because he almost caught us listening. We could not stop from laughing as we tried to make it look like we did not know what was going on. Ray was hilarious; his face was as red as a ripe tomato.

When mom called for Ray to come back in the bathroom, telling him Dad was undressed and ready now. Ray looked straight at us and said, "I'm not going back in there; Dad doesn't have any clothes on." "No kidding" we said, still trying to muffle our laughter and convincing him at the same time he was the only one that could lift Dad so hurry up and get back in there poor Dad was getting cold. "Alright," he said, "but you guys owe me." He certainly was not happy, but he was a trooper and started to go back in.

Now this part still makes me laugh as I pictured it happening all over again. As Ray opened the bathroom door and went in, we heard him tripping and bumping into everything. We were tempted to peek in to see what was happening but we knew he would yell at us and probable quit. So we quietly listen at the door trying to figure out what was going on. As soon as we heard mom say to Ray, while laughing, why do you have your eyes closed, we got the picture and almost lost it. Even Dad started laughing at him as he said, "come on Ray open your eyes, I'm not going to bite you. Don't you think it would be a lot easier if you could see what you're doing?"

It was becoming harder and harder for us to compose ourselves from not laughing loudly, fully knowing Ray would say, "that's it, if you guys think it's so funny then you get in here." We certainly didn't want to do that.

The next thing we heard was Ray grunting as he struggled to use the transfer board to sliding Dad onto the shower chair. We figured Ray was starting to settle down a bit as we heard him climb into the tub behind Dad so he could use the shower hose to get Dad all wet. Finally, Ray figured it would be easier to open his eyes although making sure with a loud voice that he was not looking directly at Dads exposed body parts. At the same time, making sure mom did not leave the bathroom. The roar of mom's laughter got louder and louder. Of course, we girls were still trying to hold back our laughter wasn't helping the situation either.

After Dad was all wet it was time to soap him down. Ray did not have a problem doing that, but only to a certain point. He then stopped and looked over at mom with a very loud excited voice again, saying, "Okay that's it, I've had it I'm done, the rest of the washing is your job mom! I am not going to touch Dad's private parts, you are his wife and you're used to that. Let me out of here before you do that!" At that point, we all lost it. We couldn't hold back our laughter any longer, especially Dad. He was laughing so hard he almost fell off the shower chair. In the end, we all knew Ray had to go back in to move Dad to the wheelchair but he was done with everything else, mom had to get him dress. What a scene that became, it looked like it came right out of a comedy show.

Moments like those kept us laughing, helping us to get through the day. Always taking one day at a time, that is how we managed. You know Ray never got used to Dad's shower routine. He still went into the bathroom with his eyes closed. However, he did get better he did not **TRIP** anymore.

Then it was our turn. Most of the time there were four of us girls to help, my sisters Linda, Mary, Karen our sister-in-law and I. Since we were not as strong as Ray, we always needed two of us around all the time.

I fondly remember another funny episode a couple of us girls managed to get ourselves into caring for Dad. It too, turned out to be hilarious.

As I remember, Karen and I were the only girls there on this particular day. Normally other family members were always popping in and out of the house all day long. I guess everyone felt Dad was safe so it was a good opportunity for everyone to be caught up in their own homes.

We knew we were on our own which did not bother us. At this point in his illness, it was easy for us. We figured we were there mostly to keep him company. Soon we found out how fast that changed.

Our episode could have easily turned into trouble fast, luckily, for us it only ended up with a lot of shared laughter. My only regret was I wished we could have captured the moment on video tape so the whole family could have enjoyed it along with us. I know they would have gotten a good laugh out of it. It was one of those moments just telling the story was not half as funny as being there. At least it was our special moment to share, which I never forgot.

You see the reason why Karen and I were there that day was it was Wednesday, mom's grocery shopping day. For her that routine was always on the same day. Unfortunately, it was a routine that eventually just faded away the sicker Dad became. In fact, nothing for her would ever become normal again, which was very sad for mom.

Mom was so funny with her grocery shopping; it was the highlight of her day. She never needed much; after all it was just her, Dad and Ray. Since there were no more family Sunday dinners, she did not have to buy for us. In fact, dinners in the house became TV dinners, unless one of us cooked something and brought it over. Grocery day was just a chance for her to get out of the house. Now more than ever she needed that outlet. She knew everyone who worked in the grocery store on a first name bases. When mom walked into the store everyone would say, "Hi Mrs. Gutherie, how are you doing"? She always ate that up with everyone recognizing her. She enjoyed being popular, it made her feel important. It was something her and Dad always shared when he was working, since he was up in the ranks in

Ford Motor Company, everyone knew Dad and because of that, mom to was noticed. We used to call her Mrs. Queen Bee. It was a position she enjoyed.

Living in a small community, everyone knew about Dad's illness. They always took the time to ask how Dad was doing. It was no wonder she took so long to grocery shopping. She enjoyed all the conversations she was having.

When Dad became worse, she never had the desire to go out anymore. Even if mom wanted to get out of the house, it was not easy for her to get into the car and go; she never had a driver's license. She always depended on someone to take her. I never knew the reason why she never got one.

We were all sitting in the kitchen one morning with mom and Dad when mom asked, "who wants to take me to the grocery store?" Usually it was my daughter Kim's job. Kim loved the special bond she had with mom, but she was in school.

It did not take Ray long at all to jump up and volunteer, especially with Karen and me there. He said, "I can, the girls are here, and they are very capable of staying alone with Dad. After all, they keep on gloating about those instructions they took, since their still rubbing it in. They keep saying it gave them all kinds of confidence to help with Dad, so this is a good chance for them to prove it. After all, we're just going to the store how long can that take, as he shot us this gloating grin at us.

Deep down inside Ray knew he finally found a way to get back at us for laughing at him with that bathroom episode he had with Dad. He was ready for some paybacks and this in his eyes this was a perfect opportunity. Although, he knew that if Dad was really going to need help, he would have never left us alone. He did not want paybacks that badly. Karen and I shot him this grin right back and said "you go right ahead Ray and don't you worry we do have this under control."

Again, Ray said to Dad before he left, "are you sure you don't need to lie down before I go"? Dad replied "no, I want to sit here with the girls and talk a little longer, I know you and mom won't take too long," so off they went.

Nevertheless, they were gone for quite awhile and Dad was starting to get impatient because his bottom was getting sore. Even at this early stage in his illness we still had to be careful he did not get any sores on his bottom from pressure of sitting too long. We were aware if that type of a sore broke the skin, infections could set in and cause all types of problems. At least we did our homework on that issue.

Looking at Dad, we could tell he was getting uncomfortable. We did not know how much longer they were going to be. We told him, "don't be foolish, if you're getting sore you need to get some pressure off your butt. We're going to help you get into bed so you can lie down."

As we wheeled Dad down the hall to his bedroom, trying to reassure him this was not going to be a problem; we can get you into bed by ourselves. You could tell by the look on Dad's face that we were not convincing him enough. I think I was trying to convince myself at the same time however; I tried not to show Dad my concerns.

Our strategy was just like Rays, we had a plan also. We positioned the wheelchair sideways next to the bed removing the arms of the chair for easier access and locking the wheels in place to prevent the chair from moving. Now it was in the ready position for our next step. Dad still felt a little uneasy about all of this so he said, "now girls lets talk about this, shouldn't we wait for Ray to get home." I know he was a little nervous with us since this was our first time attempting this.

Again I tried to reassure him, "Dad, we didn't take all those classes for nothing; we did pay attention, now it's time for us to put them to work. Don't worry we are very capable of doing this," as I looked over at Karen and said, "aren't we"? She just smiled nervously and said, "I think so."

It was on with our challenge we were ready. Even though I was a little nervous, I tried hard not to show it. I figured the worst case scenario was if he falls it was not far. He could not hurt himself because I would have softened the fall with my body although, I could be crushed, but he would be okay.

Karen was a very tiny woman but very strong and mighty. She claimed her strength came from taking karate classes, which we heard repeatedly. I figured now she could finally prove it to me.

As we worked on our plan of action, so-to-speak, Karen decided she was going to stand up on the bed right behind Dad's pillows. That way she could position him back on to the bed right next to them, while using the belt that I was going to put around Dad's waist to lift and pull him into place. Of course standing on the bed to implement this plan was not part of our instructions that was Karen's great idea. I had to make her feel like she was part of the planning also. My part was going to be sliding Dad from the wheelchair to the bed using this transfer board, which looked like it was going to work out great. Of course, I had the easiest job.

As we started to act on our plan, first I had to put this very wide belt around Dad's waist to help with the lifting process. I was amazed the advantage it gave me. Then as I glided Dad along this transfer board moving his legs at the same time while lifting them onto the bed, Karen would grab onto Dad's belt pulling him up onto the bed. In my mind it look liked a piece of cake!!!!

Only one problem we faced, which I never knew I was going to encounter, Dad was very ticklish. Even before I had a chance to get this belt around his waist, he started laughing. When I tried it again it only made him laugh some more. Just the thought of me touching his side made him explode with laughter. You know how they say laughter is contagious, well it was getting to the point it was hard for Karen and I to compose ourselves because we started laughing along with Dad. It got to the point, when I finally got the belt around his waist; I had to wipe the tears from his eyes because he was laughing so much. By this time, you would have thought mom and Ray would have been home. That was not happening, so it was on with the next step.

I think Dad was getting a little more nervous now, looking up at Karen on the bed as he said, "now look gals, really I don't mind if we wait for Ray to get home, I'm not too sore. I don't think we're going to be able to do this."

Again I said, "Dad we can do this! I told you we did not take those classes for nothing, as my voice got a little louder and assertive." "Okay", I said to Dad, "now you have to stop laughing so I can get this belt buckled." After I had it buckled, I looked over at Karen who was in a ready position on the bed to do her part and said, "on the count of three we can do this. "Are you ready Karen?" All she could do was giggle and say, "I guess so," trying to keep her balance because the bed was bouncing a lot and she didn't want to lose her footing and fall.

Seeing Karen trying to stay balanced was making Dad even more nervous. I reassured him everything is fine, then I proceeded to start counting, "okay hear we go," Karen leaned over to get ready to grab Dad's belt to pull him up. As I counted, "1-2-3 go," I couldn't believe it we did it, yelling with excitement! I was so proud of us. "What team work," I said gleaming with accomplishment.

No sooner, did I say that Karen tried to position Dad on to his pillow he fell backwards causing Karen to lose her balance and fall down on top of him. It is a good thing she was a tiny Lady and did not weigh much to cause Dad any harm. I could not do anything to help her because I was fighting hard not to let Dad's feet slide off the bed. If they did, he could have tumbling down with them and my fear of being crushed could have really happened.

Dad was laughing so hard with everything all he could say with his **great sense of humor**, "Karen, you better get up fast or you could be in big trouble when mom comes home and catches you lying on top of me." Well, you should have seen Karen; she jumped up so fast with her face all blushed with embarrassment, while Dad and I could not stop laughing. Nevertheless, we finally calmed down and got Dad situated in bed just before mom and Ray came home. When they asked, "were there any trouble?" We just looked at each other and said, "of course not," and started laughing all over again, proving that laughter was indeed the best medicine.

CHAPTER 19
Home care vs. Nursing Home

Unfortunately, like everything else with Dad's illness his simple routines disappeared fast. Sadly, we were constantly making adjustments. His disease rapidly progressed to the point when he was sitting up he had to be propped up with all kinds of pillows. Remember his equilibrium problem well it was gone. All it took was one bounce of the bed making him tip and fall on his side, or even worse, fall off the bed. We had to go back to the drawing board to learn how to care for him differently with this new phase in his illness, which was sad for us to see. We were still in denial and did not want to admit he was getting worse.

The hardest thing for me to watch was the way the little grandkids had to adjust to Dad's new situation. It was so hard to keep them off the bed. They were used to getting up on the bed to interact with grandpa. Being as active as they were we now had to monitor them. They did not understand why they could not sit on grandpa's bed anymore asking us "how can we give grandpa hugs?" We certainly did not want to discourage that, but now we had to lift them up and hold them so there was no bouncing of the bed.

After awhile they became bored with the whole thing. Even if Dad tried to make them feel comfortable by making jokes why they could not climb on the bed on their own, only made them skittish as they shied away from it completely. Of course, they never stopped talking to grandpa as they ran from one part of the house to another. In a sad way grandpa just became a part of the fixtures to them in the room.

We tried to make light of this hoping to avoid disturbing feelings about coming to mom and Dad's house. Their house needed the sounds of children playing. It helped to cheer everyone up. It was hard enough trying to keep some type of family normalcy in their house as it was.

Thank goodness, kids will be kids no matter what happens. The changes did not seem to bother the little ones too much. After all, they were not used to seeing grandpa home all the time. It was a lot different with the older grandchildren. They had a lot of adjusting to overcome.

As Dad's disease progressed, again it was back to the adjustments for everyone. Now something was happening to his breathing. The doctors did warn us about the necessity to keep him mobile because of pneumonia setting in his lungs. We thought we had a handle on that; we were focusing on moving him back and forth from the bed to the wheelchair all the time, so why was his breathing becoming a problem, we were doing exactly what they said to do.

I have to admit trying to stay one-step ahead of his next phase with this disease was changeling. For me, I needed to feel I was doing the best I could, it was the only way mentally I could handle everything Dad was going through. Thank goodness at this point in his illness he was still able to talk with us when he had a problem. At least we were not playing guessing games.

Everyday we were facing a new crisis. With the muscles gone from Dad's lower back it was causing him to be very uncomfortable sitting in his chair for long periods. Relieving the pressure by placing pillows under his bottom all the time was necessary. It was the only way to prevent open sores, which could turn into serious infections. However, we had to keep him moving back and forth to help with his lungs too. As we tried to take care of one problem, another one would pop up.

Simple routines for his care were starting to fade away. Now we were concerned with infections setting in, since it was obvious his immune system was weaker, what could possibly happen next?

As fast as Dad's disease was progressing, we started to be afraid of his next phase. Could this mean he could not get out of the bed anymore? Could this mean his lungs were collapsing? All of those were impossible for us to fathom. Our hands were tied not knowing where to turn.

Yes, Dad's care was becoming harder for us to do after all; we were not professional health caretakers. It was starting to wear us down, but to give up was not in our nature even now. I kept on thinking repeatedly how important it was now more than ever, that Dad needed us.

I know our own families were starting to have a hard time with us being gone all the time, even though they never put any restrictions on us. We still couldn't entertain the thought of alternative care for Dad. Now we're caught in the middle with major decisions.

Nevertheless, mom knew what was ahead of us, as she remembered what she went through caring for grandma many years ago. Now she was doing the same things with Dad fully knowing what was going to happen in the end. It is no wonder mom started to mention getting some professional help with caring for Dad at home, but we were still against it. To us, that only meant one thing having strangers helping. Every time she tried to convince us, we had a fit. Mom knew this was a sensitive subject for us. She was only trying to stay a step ahead with what was yet to come with Dad's care.

To be honest with you no matter how much mom tried to convince us professional home care would help, nothing was going to change our minds, at least not yet. Blinded by our love and devotion with the strong bond that fathers and daughters shared, and realizing how many years Dad was there for us, we felt it was our turn; at least we owed that to our Dad. Having strangers come in to take care of him was unthinkable for us. Yes, I know we were fooling ourselves trying to prove we could do it all. Reacting with our hearts and not our minds only gets everyone caught up in the moment.

All of this is now hindsight. Especially as we realize what kind of responsibility, it is to take care of a loved one by yourself, or even with family helping. Eventually it becomes a feeling of a trapped situation. It can turn even the best relationships into a love-hate one and that is not fair for you or your loved one.

YES, there is no doubt it will take a toll on the caretaker, and when they start to fall apart, who takes care of them? I saw it happen with mom, even though we were there with her every step of the way, it mentally tore her apart and brought her down. At the time when you are directly, involved you do not realize it until its too late. No one can tell you how it is going to turn out.

Yet, even knowing that each phase we took with Dad's care we struggled to make the best of it, and we tried hard to overcome every situation we ran into. Ultimately, our laughter did turn into tears as his care became more serious and harder for us to do by ourselves.

One thing I did regret though, we all went home to normal families and normal lives, but mom was there 24 hours a day. There was not any normalcy for her anymore. She never left the house unless it was to go to the grocery store. Yes, it was always her choice because we encouraged her to do things outside of the house from time to time, for her own peace of mind. I truly think if she decided to do that, it would have made her feel like she was deserting Dad. I guess in a sense you could say they both became homebound.

Mom was a type of person that took the oath we all said when we got married, "for better or for worse," to heart. Knowing it was her duty but feeling guilty, she could not or even wanted to care for Dad anymore.

She was burn out and rundown. Never wanting to let us, girls know mentally she could not take it anymore. It became obvious when it started to show in other ways.

Consequently, we focused on keeping Dad healthy making sure he was care for; and never realized how mom was falling apart. If only we had not been so blind. I cannot imagine how we overlooked her situation. I know the stress was really starting to get to us and we were not around 24 hours a day. Like I said Dad was helpless, and that is all we saw.

Unfortunately, mom's outlet became her drinking. It became a way to release her inner stress. I know she and Dad used to drink together socially, but this was different. Yet, we let her. In our minds, we justified it in a way; that maybe it made her feel better. In our eyes, it was better than being on any type of drugs, although eventually it did start to get out of hand. When we questioned her about her drinking, she would quickly snap back a comment to let us know it was to help her get a good night's rest so she could help with Dad's care the next day. In reality, we knew it was only an excuse. As long as it did not look like it was going to cause any harm to her or Dad with Ray still living at home we felt safe ignoring it.

I have said before there was no road map to follow with this disease. Our journey along this road was becoming very bumpy with no guidance, and nowhere to turn. We were on our own.

When I think about what she had to handle, I cannot imagine being in her shoes. Mom was losing the man she spent most of her life with, her husband, her companion of 40 years. It was more than she could bear.

The bottom line was it did take a toll overall. Our life, our loving family we once knew, no longer existed. Togetherness never happened again, at least not like it did in the past. It's no wonder some family members had a hard time dealing with all of this. Dad's disease caught us all off guard. We never had time to adjust.

CHAPTER 20
Arming ourselves with knowledge

I will never forget when my sister Linda first heard about Dad's illness. She was in denial from the very start. Dad was her rock, as he was ours too. Although it was different with Linda, she seemed to lean on him the most.

When Linda was a teenager, we all used to tease her about how much she had Dad wrapped around her finger. It was obvious to us especially when Linda would get away with things the rest of us would have gotten into big trouble for. There was a strong bond between them. It certainly gave her the motivation to find anything or anyone that could help us fight this deadly disease.

When Linda was determined with anything she did, she always went full steam ahead. Moreover, at this moment she was more than just determined, she became mad and was not going to take Dad's illness sitting down. I was very glad to see her get that upset. We all needed some other type of distraction. Linda aggressively went at this disease with the attitude the more knowledge we had possibly could lead to other alternative treatments. Never did she leave any stone unturned.

When she was researching, she came across a neurologist here in Michigan who was familiar with A.L.S. With an extra plus for us, he even was working in a hospital in Detroit, which was close to home. He not only became Dad's doctor but our family advisor too. Now we had some help, someone to show us the way, finally a road map to follow. Even though at this point his hands were tied, we still had a professional we could lean on, which took a lot of burden off the family. He never hesitated in helping us with anything for Dad's care. He truly was a great compassionate man.

I remember one day when Linda came across an article she read about homeopathic health treatments for neurological diseases. Of course, A.L.S. really got her attention when she read it. When she showed it to me my first thought was what in the world was homeopathic health, even though it has been around for many years I never heard of it until now.

Linda showed the article to Dad, I could not believe how everything started to fall into place. After he read it, he was in deep thought with this question on his face. Then he said to mom, "isn't Marian who was the wife of one of the engineers who worked for Dad, up on this type of knowledge?" Mom said, "as a matter of fact I think I do remember her talking about it before. I always had a tendency to pretend I was interested in it just to be polite. It certainly would not hurt to give her a call and get her input on this." We were all excited we had found another avenue to help us with Dad's illness. At least it made us feel like we were doing something.

Marian was so excited when she received Dad's call. If there was something for Dad in that field, she was the person who could find it. She was a great inspiration for Dad especially with her bubbling personality and a never giving up attitude. I think that is why they always got along. If nothing else came out of this her coming out to the house twice a week lifted his spirit. She was even doing this in her spare time because she was still working as a nurse, which also became helpful to us.

Now we had two professional people on our side. We were armed and ready to attack this disease. We figured with this new direction for Dad certainly could not hurt anything. After all we kept hearing repeatedly from the medical field themselves, there still was not enough knowledge about A.L.S., so what did we have to lose.

However, I have always questioned that statement. Hasn't this disease been around for a long time? I felt the reality was if someone famous came down with A.L.S., they would get the attention and then it would bring more awareness to this disease. Don't get the wrong idea, I think that's a good thing, but why does it take someone famous to do that? There are people who aren't famous dying from this disease, no matter who you are we need the help.

Marian was hilarious with her bubbly attitude when she came out to their house. She set Dad up with all types of herbs she made drinkable for him. She also put him on a regimen of all types of vitamins. I used to laugh at the way she bossed Dad around. I can still here her say right now. "Now Al", she would say, "you know this is good for you, even if it does not taste good. Do you think I would give you something that was not safe? Now, drink up." She always made him laugh as she bossed him around.

As we started to learn more about alternative health we always passed it on to Dad's doctor first to make sure it did not cause him any harm, we were very cautious with that. To our surprise he never thought it was a waste of time or that we were foolish pursuing other avenues besides modern medicine. Being a neurologist with an open mind was a plus for us.

One day with Linda researching, she came across this article on a hair analysis. The article sounded very interesting as it explained what the test was used for. That's what got her attention. Through this test, they stated they could tell how much toxic chemical buildup there was in your system. The more we read about it the more we realized how toxins could cause this destruction on your body. It was amazing we never realized that before, but it certainly made sense.

What really got our attention was the article went on to say if they did find harmful chemicals in your system they could possibly rid the body of them with a process called chelating. Then hoping the nervous system would respond to the treatment. Of course, we fully knew this was all speculation a wild guess, but right now, it did not matter to us, we were still willing to try anything.

However, if there were already permanent damage done to the nervous system then we would have another issue to deal with. For now, we figured we would cross that bridge when we got there. We just wanted to relish in the fact we found something very interesting. Not knowing what was going to happen with the process we dealt with it one-step at a time. There is no doubt we were always playing the waiting game to see what would happen next. Even though time was not on our side we had the patience.

When Linda called the doctor to ask if this could be done on Dad he responded, "I'm willing to give it a try to see what happens." Especially knowing where Dad worked all his life in the automotive industry and exposed too many types of chemicals.

Our minds immediately started focusing on the "what-ifs." Maybe if it turned out that a certain type of chemical did show up in his body perhaps it was responsible for triggering his A.L.S. We imagined all types of possibilities. Even though we had something else to focus on for a while, I never let my guard down.

As we thought back to what type of chemicals Dad was exposed to, I remembered reading about a possibility of toxic chemicals in an article in a homeopathic magazine about shots he had to have when he went to Germany. It certainly put a lot of emphasis on the harm they could possibly do to your system, even to this day, 2011; the debate is still on going.

Only a week went by since we submitted a piece of Dad's hair for this test although it felt like eternity, we could not wait to get the results back. We were hopeful this was going to be the answer to our prayers. We really needed that right now for Dad was running out of time.

Our focus was going in the direction of maybe if we found what was causing Dad's disease possibly it could lead to a treatment to slow it down, or better yet, cure it. Even though the odds were against us, if something were to happen it truly would have been a miracle. I felt we were due. Now it was obvious Dad's breathing was getting worse, which was scaring us, so a miracle couldn't happen soon enough. Even his swallowing was becoming an issue, which soon meant his food had to be in a liquid form. Knowing that we didn't have a lot of time before Dad could no longer eat, only urged Jim and I to celebrate Dad's birthday early by taking him out to dinner while he could still enjoy solid foods, never realizing it was going to be his last real meal.

We knew he loved this quaint little restaurant right down the street from where they lived so we wanted to take them there. Back in his healthier days it was one of his favorite places to go because they had crab legs every Friday. Man did Dad love his crab legs! It is one of Jim's favorite meals also.

Back in Dad's healthier days when we all went out to dinner and they both order, "all you could eat crab legs," it took forever for them to finish. Since I was finished way before them I got bored sitting there waiting. Of course they both took advantage of "all you could eat."

At first Dad was a little hesitant to go, since he could not walk or could not use his hands anymore unfortunately you had to help him. That really disturbed him being out in public. However, that did not concern Jim. As he told Dad not to worry, "we will go when they first open up so there won't be many people there, and we will take our time so you have a chance to enjoy your meal. I will even help to feed you, believe me I don't mind doing this. Anyway I have this craving for crab legs myself," so off we went.

I cannot tell you how proud I was of Jim that day. When the dinner came to the table, Dad and Jim had two huge plates of crab legs. You could see Dad's eyes get big as the smell excited him. As Jim proceeded to feed Dad, I could not help noticing how Jim's crab legs got cold. I offered to help but he wanted to do this for Dad. After Dad was full, Jim ate his meal and not once complained about them being cold. It was that day when I realized how much affection and love Jim had for Dad. For Jim to give up a warm plate of crab legs there had to be a special reason.

CHAPTER 21
Our hope and despair on the same day

I was over at mom and Dad's house one morning sitting with Dad while he was eating breakfast. The phone rang and mom leaped to answer it. I know she was anxiously waiting for the doctor's call when the phone ranged. All she said when she answered the phone was, "hi doctor," then there was silence. You could see this intense look on her face as she was listening. I just held my breath waiting for her to say something. I could feel my heart pounding. When I looked over towards Dad, I saw he was in a trance also trying to listen to mom's conversation. The doctor was telling her about the results of Dad's hair analysis test. I was so glad I was there to hear this news first hand that memory of excitement in Dad's face was priceless.

When she hung up the phone mom started crying uncontrollably all she could say was "the doctor said," then she started calming down somewhat so she could finish her sentence. "He wants Dad down at the hospital as soon as possible." As I sat there in a stupor waiting for her to continue the rest of their conversation, I felt myself holding my breath. Then with excitement in her voice, she blurted out "Dad's test showed high toxic levels of aluminum and mercury in his blood." The excited look on Dad's face after mom told us was overwhelming. We all started screaming and crying with joy.

Now do not get the wrong idea we weren't happy to hear Dad had a high level of toxic chemicals in his blood stream. We were cautiously excited thinking that maybe we finally hit upon something positive.

Even hoping that maybe this is what triggers his disease. In our way of thinking now, you have a cause, so now you can find a way to attack the problem. It's as simple as that. Our minds and thoughts were racing so much; that we even had this vision of a medical breakthrough unfolding right before our eyes. Our Dad was going to be part of history, so we thought!

Mom continued, "the doctor said there was no doubt in his mind the necessity of him having the chelation therapy done as soon as possible." Then he explained how they were going to do it. Of course cautioning, us at the same time this was experimental so don't get your hopes up. They did not know how successful this treatment would be with removing the chemicals from the body. On the other hand, if it was successful there was no way to tell how his body would respond to it. To us that did not matter we were just excited to hear he was willing to try this.

Talk about excitement in the house. We were screaming and crying at the same time it was time to celebrate! We finally hit upon some hope to hold on to. In our eyes, we were already thinking this was going to help Dad. Our excitement was contagious. I even saw Dad's eyes tear up. Could this be the answer to our prayers? I tell you what that phone call could not have come at a better time.

It was late July 1985, and Dad's birthday was coming up in August. We thought what a great birthday present this was going to be for him if it was successful, although we were still very concerned with his breathing.

Dad's lungs were reacting as if he was coming down with a bad cold or even worse, pneumonia. You could see his chest go up and down from trying to take deep breaths. He kept on saying he feels a lot of pressure on his chest as if something heavy was sitting on him.

Not knowing anything about this disease, we never felt it was the disease doing this. Therefore, in all fairness to the family we never prepared ourselves for what lied ahead of us.

Excitedly we were all prepared to go to the hospital along with Dad that morning pilling into a van that had a wheelchair lift that his engineers from work converted over for him. Just then, I started to realize this might be our last chance, our last hope to stop the destruction to Dad's body. Releasing this big sigh of relief feeling like this huge burden just lifted off our shoulders, wondering to myself if our nightmare, our battle, was finally ending.

It was then I realized this was a major turning point for Dad. Thinking everything was finally going to be ok**ay.** It is amazing how right I was, as you will read. Yes, it was a **major** turning point for Dad; unfortunately, **one that only enhanced his demise!**

The ride to the hospital was quite enjoyable as Ray, Linda, mom and I got into the van fighting over who was going to sit near Dad. Laughing and carrying on just as we used to telling jokes as if nothing ever happened to him, enjoying the beautiful sunshine along the way. Cautiously making sure Dad did not laugh too much because every time he did he looked like he was going to lose his breath.

It became hard not to let your guard down. Even though we were cautiously being positive it was a feeling we never wanted to let go. It had been awhile since we were that excited, we all needed that spark, especially Dad.

Our excitement even got to the point that we made dinner reservations for the ride home, since the doctor told us this process would probably take most of the day we figured it would be a great way to celebrate. I just wished I could have found a way to embrace that moment forever. Even finding a way to bottle it up somehow so I could open it up on the days when I felt completely desolate.

When we arrived at the hospital, we were not there very long when all our dreams and hopes vanished into mid air. All our emotions came crashing down. Sadly, there was no safety net to catch us. We felt stranded and did not know which way to turn.

Here we were sitting in the hospital waiting area patiently waiting for Dad to start his treatment. Having fun and telling jokes still, when it only seemed like seconds, Dad started choking from laughing so hard. It was obvious to us he could not catch his breath. You should have seen the action in the waiting room responding to him. I think a whole army of doctors and nurses stampeded in to get to him. They rushed Dad out so fast we did not know what happened to him.

Before we realized what hit us, here we were **again** sitting outside the intensive care room waiting to hear something about Dad. It felt like forever until we saw someone who could give us an update on what just happened to him.

It felt like déjà vu. We were now facing this terrible unknown with Dad's illness. Mom, Ray, and Linda, and I were in the waiting room pacing back and forth in a state of shock, not knowing if we would ever see Dad alive again. Poor Ray, I know he did not want to be in the same situation like before when we were at the Mayo Clinic when all hell broke out. Mentally, I didn't think he was strong enough. If he had any idea this was going to happen, I know he would have stayed home.

For the first time I felt this sense of despair and hopelessness coming over me. Something I knew I could no longer handle alone. All I could think of was getting a hold of Jim. At that point, I needed him by my side to comfort me. When I finally reached Jim on the phone and told him with a quivering voice that Dad was in the intensive care unit and no one told us what was going on. He could not believe it. "That can't be happening," he said "you guys were just going down for his treatment. What in the hell happened?" It seemed like by the time I hung up the phone Jim was at the hospital.

Just then, the doctor came out and told us Dad was out of danger and was resting. **Oh my God, did we explode when he said out of danger,** especially Linda and I. "What do you mean **DANGER?**" We said! The doctor continued to say, "your Dad's breathing became stressed to the point it caused him to have a serious panic attack, putting a lot of stress on his heart. I want to keep him over night to make sure he will be strong enough to do the chelation test in the morning." After calming down, we realized what a blessing it was we were at the hospital when Dad had this attack. If he was at home, we could have lost him.

Finally, we were able to see Dad and we all agreed he was safe and out of trouble. His breathing was back to normal, so hesitantly we went home. Still our family did not know his breathing was still in danger. What happened to us next made us feel as if we were in a whirlwind turning and turning until we were so dizzy we did not know what direction to take?

The next morning Linda and mom were the first ones at the hospital. Sill hoping he was going to have the chelation treatment, knowing it was going to be an all day process they brought some games to keep Dad occupied. When they arrived, they saw he was not in his room. Panicking, Linda rushed down to the nurse's station demanding someone tell her where Dad was and what happened to him. It was then they found out Dad transferred to a step down intensive care unit in the middle of the night, his breathing was in danger again, Linda and mom lost it. The more they found out what happened to Dad the more Linda's voice became louder trembling with fear. "Why weren't we notified," she said. Mom tried to calm her down so her comments were not out of control.

I know Linda was feeling guilty she did not spend the night in the hospital with Dad. I know she was thinking about the last episode we had with him, while it was at a different hospital, the outcome could have easily caused his death if someone was not there with him. It just happened it was Jim and I with Dad that day. All I can say **thank goodness I did my homework.**

We were admitting Dad into the hospital because of a blood clot that had broken lose in his blood stream traveling through his lungs; thank goodness it passed through his heart and did not do any damage we were very fortunate. Since Dad was immobile now, being in the wheelchair or in bed most of the time, the doctor decided to give him medication to thin his blood. He said this was normal procedure when patients become less active. It is a safety precaution to prevent blood clots. Now it is important to monitor his blood so it does not cause another problem, like out of control bleeding.

When the doctor put Dad on Coumadin, he informed the family of the necessity of knowing about this medication and the danger of counteracting with other drugs. He asked us to watch a video giving us all the information we needed on it. As I watched the video I paid strict attention to the do not use list of medications with this drug, noticing that aspirin was on the top of the list. The video went on to explain that an aspirin thins the blood also, and the two together could cause heavy bleeding, to the point of causing death. This certainly got my attention.

Shortly after viewing the video, Jim and I went back to Dad's room to find him complaining of discomfort. The nurse who was in the room with us said "I will be right back to bring you something to make him feel comfortable." When she came back with this pill and a glass of water, I noticed she had an aspirin in her hand, so I nicely questioned her about it. "Isn't that an aspirin you have in your hand," I asked. As Jim tried to hush me up rolling his eyes at the same time, saying, "Pam, let the nurse do her job." However, she snapped a response back at me and said, "yes it's for your Dad's discomfort." I was so upset that I was steaming on the inside, but calmly reminded her Dad was on Coumadin and I just saw this video about the warnings of counteracting with other drugs. Aspirin was on the top of the list. Then in an assertive voice, I told her maybe you should check his chart better!" Jim hung his head down thinking to himself I was out of line with my comment. The nurse picked up Dad's chart and read it and said, ***"wow,* you're right,"** and walked out of the room to get a Tylenol. Never saying, "I'm sorry, my mistake," or even thanking me because she could have gotten into big trouble from the doctors, just walked out of the room.

I was so upset I shot this eye-piercing look at Jim making a comment at the same time saying, "let this be a lesson for all of us, especially you! Please don't ever be afraid to ask questions, especially if I'm laying there in the hospital bed helpless!" Remember these professionals are human they can make mistakes too.

It scares me to think if we were not there to ask questions, Dad may have had the aspirin on top of the Coumadin and could have bled to death. Right then it confirmed my beliefs to always ask questions and be your own advocate. It was a lesson well learned that did not turn out to be a catastrophe.

As mom and Linda proceeded to find out what room Dad was in they found him tired and stressed out but very relieved to see them. He told them he had a very rough night. It was obvious to them he was still struggling with his breathing. Not knowing at the time it was still putting a lot of stress on his heart. I guess we should have been more assertive in asking the doctors more questions about his problem, because we were all baffled why he was struggling so much.

I know the doctors were cautious about revealing anything to us until they knew what they were dealing with. They kept reminding us each patient is affected differently. Without any guidance and not having a step-by-step map to follow on what was going to happen next with Dad's illness we were totally unprepared.

Therefore, we had to put our trust and faith in the doctors and hope for the best. At least in our hearts we knew Dad was in the right place especially with everything that was going on with him, as we still tried to concentrate on our main objective, getting him stronger so he could still have the chelation process done.

This whole time Linda could not shake this strange feeling that something was not right with Dad. Trying to keep his mind occupied by playing games was not helping her or Dad. You could tell his mind was going 100 miles an hour trying to figure out what was going on with his breathing, and was very concerned about not being able to have the chelation test, especially realizing the cleansing of his blood from these toxin may be his last hope just made him panic even more. He was concentrating so hard on not talking, hoping it would keep his breathing under control. Nevertheless, the more he thought about them canceling the test the more anxious he became. I know deep down inside he knew it was not going to do anything although; he could not help believing in hope!

Dad got himself so worked up thinking about all of this, that Linda and mom thought it would be better if they left the room for a little while so he could calm down. As they got up to go down to the waiting room, Dad started to panic, struggling to try to tell them something. Mom thought he was concerned that they were leaving as she tried to reassure him they were not going far, just to the waiting room for a cup of coffee; and they would not be gone long.

I remember Linda saying when they returned to Dad's room they noticed he was in a high stress situation as they found him gasping for air. Mom started yelling for someone to come into the room while panicking and pressing the help button at the same time. However, there was no response. Linda was not wasting any time she ran down to the nurse's station to find someone. Finally, in desperation Dad was able to muster up a long enough breath to tell them "quick get my doctor, hurry I can't breathe!" When his doctor came into the room, all hell broke out. You could hear him yelling at the nurses. All of a sudden, they rushed Dad down to the intensive care area. Everything seemed to happen so fast that mom and Linda did not even get a chance to ask any questions, they just stood there **crying in dismay.**

When Ray and I arrived at the hospital, we saw the commotion leaving Dad's room. We could not believe what was happening. Everyone was hurrying in different directions. We rushed into his room. There stood mom and Linda crying uncontrollably. "What in the world is going on with Dad," I asked in a panic. All they could say was, "we don't know it happened so fast, Dad couldn't breathe."

In a flash, here we were all standing outside the intensive care section **AGAIN**. Pacing back and forth waiting for someone to come out and tell us what just happened to Dad.

I cannot tell you how many times we went through that same ordeal with our emotions. It was as if we were on a roller coaster ride constantly going up and down. This whole episode left us all of guard.

I felt bad for my brother Rick who was about 15 minutes behind Ray and I arriving at the hospital. All he saw was the tale end of the chaos coming down the hall, never thinking much about it until he walked into Dad's room, stopping dead in his tracks when he saw an empty hospital bed. I could not imagine what was going through his mind. He rushed down to the waiting room hoping to find us, his face as white as a ghost panicking while asking, "what happened to Dad where did he go?" Unfortunately, all we could say was the doctor rushed Dad to intensive care unit because he could not breathe. Rick just stood there his face expressionless. There was nothing but silence in the waiting room, which we all knew was unusual with Rick around. No one felt like talking. I think we were afraid to look at each other with fear of losing control.

It felt like hours before the doctor came out to tell us what happened to Dad. The reality was it was only minutes. He gingerly explained to us what had happened, as you could see him trying to choose his words very carefully. I think he knew it would have caused an uncontrollable panic with us. As he proceeded to explain to us he said, "your Dad started to have chest pains again this time it did get out of control. It was all caused from a pulmonary embolism in his lung which was putting stress on his heart and his breathing."

I just stood there in dismay, listening to him as this terrible feeling of numbness took over my body. It felt like I was hearing this about someone else. This really was not happening to my Dad. Then the doctor told us our worst nightmare which none of us wanted to hear.

He said, "to prevent your Dad from going into cardiac arrest we had to put him on a temporary ventilator to help him with his breathing." All I could remember the doctor saying was a **"ventilator."** Everything else blocked out.

CHAPTER 22

A situation no one wanted, coming home on life support

As a family, we were not ready for this phase in Dad's illness. It really threw us off guard. We certainly did not have any time to prepare, let alone knowing Dad never wanted this to happen. I felt we should have armed ourselves with more knowledge to help us make the right choices. The reality was, we were not thinking of his life ending. After all, we were being cautiously positive as we were going to the hospital for what we hoped was a breakthrough cure with Dad, his chelation treatment. We never prepared ourselves for Dad to be on what the doctor's were calling a "**temporary ventilator!**"

Over and over I could not stop thinking why did the doctor choose to have Dad put on the ventilator without discussing it with the family first. We were in the waiting room the whole time; they could have come out and told us what was going to happen. When they said it was in an emergency with the possibility of losing Dad's life, right then they had to make a decision to save him. By law, they were obligated.

Before the doctor let us see Dad, he warned us about his condition. We were in shock when we walked into his room. Even now, I can still see him laying there helpless. It was so hard for us to see him that way. He had so many wires and alarms hooked up to him.

Poor mom, I felt helpless for her as she broke down crying. I could not find a way to comfort her, I to was frightened. The doctor saw the forsaken look on our faces as he tried to reassure us this was just a minor set back for Dad. Along with the pulmonalogist who was also in the room, reminding us when Dad's lungs become stronger he could come off the **"temporary respirator."** "Then he said just look at this situation as a safety net for your Dad, if something were to happen again with his breathing he would now have a backup plan.

I have to admit **temporary** was the only words the family focused on, we never paying attention to anything else. To this day, I felt the doctors misguided us. Sadly, in the end Dad never came off the ventilator. **It never became temporary.**

I have said before without having any guidance with Dad's disease was a learning process from day one. The thought crossed my mind a couple of times; did these doctors felt the same way? I know they were constantly remarking throughout Dad's illness that his progression was puzzling. They even admitted they never expected it to go this fast, so it does make you wonder.

Now, 22 years later as with find more information about this disease we have learned that with the hereditary A.L.S., each person could be afflicted differently. However, at the time, we did not have any idea.

In all fairness to our family, you can see why we were always hanging on to hope. We knew it was a neurological disease. We knew Dad was not the first patient to come down with Familial A.L.S. They could have guided us better they were the professionals!

Then I remembered even the renowned Mayo Clinic telling us, Dad's A.L.S. case did not exactly follow the textbook profile. That term will always remain a mystery to me.

I have to say, so many negative thoughts were going through my mind as I tried to figure out why the doctor let Dad get to this point. At least he could have warned us so we could have made a clearer decision together as a family. I now wonder if the family had known Dad would be facing this predicament with his lungs, only to end up on a ventilator for the rest of his life, would we have chosen differently. As I thought about that comment, I will never forget the loud hysterical discussion that was going on in his room about that same topic. As poor Dad lay in his hospital bed listening to all the chaos about this so-called temporary respiratory, where was the fairness to him?

Not only was the ventilator an issue, also was the lack of nourishment down the road with the probability of a feeding tube being inevitable. Nevertheless, it still did not stop the panic of trying to convince Dad he still had a lot of quality of life left. The louder we discussed it the more chaotic the room became, everyone crying and trying to give their opinions all at the same time, as the stress level went out of control.

The reality was, we were not thinking with our minds our hearts were getting in the way. We could not bear the thought of Dad no longer being with us. No matter how extreme his illness was, we still had Dad, how selfish was that. I do not even remember asking Dad how he felt. I know he had a hard enough time looking at our sad faces to voice his opinion.

We could not stop pleading with Dad about this ventilator, in the end it was his decision. However, what could he say as he looked over at mom crying her heart out, realizing he could not do this to her at least not now, she was not ready to let him go. He knew she was not strong enough to handle any of this yet. It just happened too fast for any of us to adjust. Dad was her life and now he was lying in bed in a state of helplessness. I could not imagine being in her shoes.

When everyone calmed down, we noticed Dad's pulmonalogist was still in the room with us. He was quietly making sure Dad was comfortable and his ventilator was working properly. I did feel bad for him because he ended up in the middle of the family's chaos. Being a professional, I am sure this was not the first time he experienced that with a family. He patiently waited until everyone had settled down before he spoke.

He was very assertive and right to the point type of a doctor, which scared me a little because I had witnessed that before with Dad's first doctor. Although this time as he spoke, he had compassion in the tone of his voice, which put us all at ease right away.

Again reassuring Dad and us, this was just a temporary setback and when his heart got stronger, he could turn off the ventilator now and then. I guess I did not hear the words now and then however; it was too late to take him off the ventilator the decision was out of our control.

As he began to explain to us exactly what Dad was going to go through with this temporary ventilator, instantly I felt relieved. This doctor was the top in this field, Dad's neurologist made sure of that. With the two of them on our side guiding us, we felt very secure. Especially when his pulmonalogist told us, it was too soon for this disease to be causing this problem to his lungs. Still confused about that comment, we never thought it was going to be an issue in the first place, but here we were.

In the beginning of Dad's illness the professionals said, the only muscle not too be affected with this disease was your involuntary muscles. Never did we ask the question "what are your involuntary muscles?" Always assuming it was the heart and lungs. Justify the definition to mean to us that you could not physically control the movement yourselves, hence the term involuntary, so we thought! For the first time his comment opened my eyes and made me stop and think about Dad's future and what we were facing down the road was terrifying.

Since these professionals were telling us everything was temporary, we were becoming more comfortable believing in it, naturally! I'm sure if they were giving us a doom and gloom scenario, we would have had a closed mind and probably not have excepted it. That's only human nature.

As Dad's pulmonalogist proceeded to explain to us what needed done with the ventilator in order for Dad to be able to breathe on his own made my heart sink. I could not believe all of the information he was giving us. Thinking to myself, we really have our hands full now. Of course, it was simple for him to say or do. As he saw the panic look on our faces and tried, his best to reassure us there would not be a problem. "You don't have to be a professional to do this," as he tried to build our confidence. All I could think of now, Dad's life is in our hands. Did we want to be responsible for that? Could we live with ourselves if something happened we caused? My head was spinning with all kinds of thoughts.

Then he showed us the process of operating the ventilator. Step by step, explaining to us that the equipment had a built in warning sensor alarm that would always let us know when Dad was not getting any air. Then he proceeded to show us how to snap the ventilator tube off his trachea, which is the tube surgically inserted into his neck in order for the air to pass by his throat to go to his lungs. Letting us know if you close it off Dad could breathe on his own, enabling him to use his voice to communicate again. It also allowed him to eat as long as the food was soft. Then looking at us he said, "doesn't that look simple." I just stood there in a daze thinking to myself "wow this is serious; Dad's life is now controlled by this machine." Then as if the doctor was reading my mind he said, "don't worry about your Dad's breathing, he will know when he is starting to struggle, then all you have to do is snap the tube back on and turn on the ventilator" It's as simple as that. This machine is your Dad's insurance; it will always be there for him when he needs it.

Looking at the expression on Dad's face it seemed like the more the doctor talked about this the more restless he became. **Did Dad have a feeling this was not going to be a temporary situation**? Was he agreeing to all of this because of us? In the end, Dad gave in and listened to his family's heartbreaking plea.

You know I still cannot help putting some of the blame on the doctors that day. All they had to say was **YES** there are signs his disease is starting to take over your Dad's lungs and not putting the word temporary in our heads. However **if it went in a different direction would we have changed our minds?**

After everything, we went through with Dad's breathing episode I could not help remembering the words of the very first doctor we saw when he gave us Dad original diagnosis **"Don't waste your time and energy trying to find other answers for it will always lead you back to the same diagnosis."** Even with those words haunting me, I could not have lived with myself if we did not pursue a second opinion.

The saddest thing about this whole episode was it all started with the trip down to the hospital for what we thought was a breakthrough treatment for Dad' illness, in essence it became his destiny. Yes, everything Dad went through with this terrible disease was horrifying. It certainly was not fair to him.

When I think about how much Dad had achieved in his life with family and career, it becomes twofold. Because now, he has achieved one more thing, "the worst illness anyone could possibly imagine." **That type of achievement he did not need!**

When we brought Dad home from the hospital he was coming home on life-support, unfortunately, it never became temporary. Dad's oxygen level dropped so fast while in the hospital, his lungs became dependent on the ventilator before we even left. At the time, Dad had no documentation about his concerns and wants with his health, and once on life support legally the doctors could not take him off. Both doctors could not believe how fast the disease took over Dad's body. No words could comfort us now, it was done; Dad was now on a ventilator for the rest of his life.

It was a shock to see how fast his life changed. Just think only 10 days ago we were going down to the hospital together, laughing and telling jokes all the way. Now our Dad was coming home attached to a machine that keeps him alive, trapped for the rest of his life.

I know we should have been preparing for this, but everything just went so fast sadly, we ran out of time. I guess the reality was we were concentrating so much on finding something that would slow down or even cure his disease; we never realized we would be facing this.

I remember when we made the appointment for Dad to have the chelation treatment done at the hospital, remarking Dad's birthday was coming soon, feeling confident nothing was going to happen to him and he was going to celebrate his best birthday ever, definitely a celebration of **LIFE!**

Yes, Dad did come home in time for his birthday only to be dependent on a machine to keep him alive. As it made him feel trapped, a prisoner in his own body. The quality of life he once knew was gone. Losing the ability to talk with his family was devastating. Talk about hitting rock bottom. **WHAT A BIRTHDAY PRESENT THAT WAS!**

If it were not for the episode in the hospital putting Dad on the temporary ventilator, maybe we would have had time to think about the consequences of life-support. Do I honestly feel if we had more time to think about his outcome, would we have chosen differently? I really don't think so, in our eyes, Dad still had quality left to his life. In our hearts, the way we justified it was he still was able to somewhat use his upper body, at least for a little while longer. It is amazing how many times we fooled ourselves pretending Dad still had quality to his life. The most devastating loss for me with all of this was, **never hearing my Dad's voice again!**

Okay, now we had to huge adjustments to make. This time we had to be sure everyone in the family was still willingly to do their part. I must say now more than ever with determination pulling together making the best out this new phase in his illness everyone agreed. Although facing this unbelievable challenge with the ventilator only meant one thing 24 **hour nursing care,** which we tried so hard to avoid at first. There was no doubt we still wanted Dad to be cared for at home.

Anyone who has ever faced this type of experience knows just how expensive this endeavor can be, especially skilled nursing and all the equipment needed just to keep Dad alive. We have heard many times this disease being refer to as a rich man's disease; we are beginning to understand why now.

Right now, the money involved to care for Dad at home was the furthest thing from our minds. Maybe Dad felt differently, being a conservative person throughout his lifetime, after all, he worked hard all his life to build up this nest egg; always making sure his family was taking care of.

Now he was the one needing the care. Dad would have done the same for any of us. Now it was our turn to take care of him. How could we not feel that way, he was our Dad, he deserved the best care we could provide for him.

You know, at one point I felt a little selfish thinking that even though my Dad was on life-support it still gave me some peace of mind to know he was still alive and with us. I know it was a sense of security I truly needed at this point, never considering how he felt. I was not ready to lose him; I needed more time to adjust. I know most of the family felt the same way. With everything all said and done, I truly felt if Dad were ready to die, he would have told the doctors. He was a very intelligent man; he knew how hard this journey was going to be, after all, he would have been there with his mom if her heart didn't give out before she couldn't breathe.

It is no doubt we were facing our biggest hurdle ever. It was time for us to regroup as we tried hard to get our composure to figure out what our next plan was. Each hurdle we went through with Dad; we dealt with and treated it as only a temporary setback, it was the only way we could handle his illness. Still trying to focus on taking it one day at a time, was working for us, so far.

With this new dilemma in Dad's illness, it was more important to reassure mom we weren't backing away. She wasn't going to do this alone, trying to remind her even though we were getting skilled nursing to help with Dads care one of us would be there everyday also..

We were hoping this would free her up to have more quality time to spend with Dad. Reminding her, there were still a lot of special moments they could share together. Even just simple things like reading the morning paper to him, which was always one of Dad's favorite morning pleasures, or sitting alongside of his bed enjoying a movie together. Even though it was becoming harder for Dad to communicate with us, there was no doubt mom always knew what he wanted or needed. If you do not know your spouse after 40 years, then there must be something terribly wrong with your relationship.

CHAPTER 23

Their home becomes a hospital stressing mom with the nursing care

Unfortunately, it did not take long for their house to become a hospital. Not only did Dad lose his normalcy, so did mom. The life she once knew especially with her day-to-day routine was gone forever. Everything in mom's house had to change to fit Dad's needs.

I remember when we switch Dad's hospital bed into their living room. Their bedroom was too small with all the new equipment we had for him. Anyways the view was so much better after all; it was all he had left to enjoy. This worked out very well because it was organized for Dad's needs, and comfortable for everyone else to enjoy with him. It never gave you a feeling of a hospital room even though the sound of the ventilator was always going.

Besides the kitchen the living room was everyone's favorite place to hang out. Having Dad feel like he was part of everything and involved with the coming and goings of everyone was important. It was a lot better than being trapped in the back bedroom all by himself as he anxiously waited for a visitor. Never did we want him to feel neglected.

Their living room had this beautiful large window overlooking the lake they lived on. Dad could watch nature at its finest while the kids were playing in the lake making him feel at times as if life was somewhat normal again. We also set up a big screen TV for him to occupy his time until bedtime; although what he enjoyed the most, was company. Everyone would mingle around the fireplace and converse among themselves while Dad would listen to their conversations. Even though he could not respond to them, it was great therapy for him just to listen to what was going on. The set up in the living room for Dad could not have worked out any better. With his care constantly monitored, there was plenty of room for company not to feel like they were in the way.

At this stage in Dad's illness not being able to communicate verbally was hard for us. Not only was that gone, but he was also loosening the movement in his hands, yet we still hung on to hope knowing he could still move his head to respond to yes or no gestures for communication. However, it was becoming harder and harder to remain focused.

As we organized almost every piece of equipment, we could possible need for Dad. It was time for our next task interviewing nurses. That was a treat. First in our eyes, no nurse was good enough to care for our Dad, but we had to make some decisions quickly. Our number one priority was they had to treat him like a human being and not like a non-functioning responding body. We needed personal care as well as expertise.

When we finally found an agency that could handle the 24-hour care he needed, then our most difficult task was to learn all about the ventilator. This was something the doctor insisted we learn just in case there was ever an emergency with Dad even as simple as a nurse not showing up. I cannot tell you how many times that happened. Not only did we have to know how to operate the ventilator, but also we had to learn how to care for Dad being on it. I cannot express deeply how to describe how difficult that was to learn, especially knowing Dad's life was in our hands.

Before he came home from the hospital, we took a quick course on how to operate the ventilator. However, to maintain Dad on this all the time naturally we didn't have the skill or the knowledge. Now we were talking about a completely new ball game.

There was so much to do just to keep Dad breathing on the ventilator, if you linger on it too much it knowing that you had Dad's life in your hands could have scared you to death. Just one simple mistake could jeopardize his breathing putting his life at risk. For instance, like clearing his throat. Saliva was consistently blocking his breathing tube causing the flow of air to slow down, or in a worst-case scenario, no air at all could get through. A simple explanation, imagine as if it was a water hose, when it's bent no water can get through even though it was turned on.

When the ventilator tech had us girls perform this procedure by ourselves, I thought I was going to get sick to my stomach. I was so nervous putting this long skinny suction hose down into Dad's trachea in his throat to vacuum up all the secretions. The whole time we were clearing this tube in his throat the connection to the ventilator was off, and he wasn't getting any air. It was as if he was holding his breathe panicking and waiting for us to hook him back onto the machine. I couldn't look at his face I was so fearful I would have lost it.

If that wasn't nerve-racking enough the whole time you were doing that the alarm on the ventilator was blaring away because Dad was not connected. Making you tense up even more as you felt the pressure of Dad's life in your hands. All of those thoughts were going through my head while I was performing this procedure were enough to make me hyperventilate. For us having our emotions involved was very frightening. Eventually we relaxed a little bit and became faster at it thank god! When I look back at that now I can't imagine doing something like that again. I know I wouldn't have had the same mental stamina.

In the end, we finally gained a lot of confidence in ourselves making us feel like we just graduated from nursing school. After that, we faced our fears with a positive attitude, as we got use to knowing Dad's life was always in our hands and we never ran away.

When I remember, what it took to be involved with his care was definitely a huge undertaking for us girls. All the work we did just to keep Dad comfortable, healthy and **alive** was unreal. Eventually it became part of our normal routine. At times, I felt we were the ones explaining to the nurses how to do this.

When I look back just thinking about the many different situations we could have encountered which could have easily cost Dad his life were overwhelming. I do not know how we endured it.

There were simple problems which no one had any control over, although could have been life threaten. For instance losing electricity during a bad storm, this would shut of the ventilator. Even though we had a back up battery, it did not stay charged for a long time use. Then your last resort was to hand bag him so he could breathe, using this hand held apparatus that looked like a balloon that you hook onto his trachea squeezing it to get air into his lungs. That incident only happened to us once. Then we learned from it by calling the power company telling them Dad's life is in danger without any power, explaining to them he was on a ventilator. From then on, we were always the first ones to have the power back on, and if it was going to be awhile before that happened they even bring out a generator for us to use.

On the other hand, situations with medication always, making sure the dosage was correct and they didn't counteract with other medication was extremely important. Never was there time to panic, we always had to be on our toes. At least one of us had to keep a level head all the time. It was a good thing we had a great team to balance that.

I was amazed with my family's attitude throughout this entire ordeal most of the time we remained positive. This was no doubt a tremendous challenge but one we knew we could handle. There's no doubt not known what was in store for us down the road helped to maintain that attitude. We weren't always looking over our shoulders.

Anyway putting our lives on hold was only temporary, Dad's disease was progressing so fast we knew it would not last forever. Being with him for what little time he had left was a blessing to us. You always find a way to endure when you have some hope to guide you along your journey. However, when it is gone either put your hands in a higher entity, or find a safe way to find your release.

Doctors have said too much stress can be the cause to a lot of illness.

Unfortunately, for mom hers was building up over the nursing care for Dad. Yes, we had nurses coming by 24 hours a day however it did not relieve her stress, you could tell it was starting to wear on her. She was a tiny and frail woman to begin with.

The saddest thing she had to cope with besides Dad's illness was her home turning into a hospital. At the end of the day, we had a home to go to sadly, mom no longer had a place she could call a home. No place could she retreat too. However, when her life turned up side down and it became uncontrollable she did find some solitude— **sadly, it was her bedroom, all alone!**

Their home, the home in which she and Dad were going to retire in slowly became a hospital with a continually revolving door. Even when she was in bed for the night, she had to trust the nurse that was coming for the midnight shift was the right one. Her door was never locked how could it you could not give all the nurses a key. It was a good thing Ray was still living at home with her at least she had some peace of mind feeling secure.

There were professionals coming and going 24 hours a day. The minute you became used to one nurse for some reason something would always happen and she never came back again. They did not tell you ahead of time that a nurse was not coming. Constantly we had to be prepared to go with the flow.

Mom's quality home time for herself was always changing. Every day became a different situation for her. Sometimes even her morning showers became afternoon ones if it happened at all. I guess in a sense you could say she never became bored and she never had to worry about being alone if that is any consolation! I am sure there were times she yearned for her own space everyone needs that now and then.

Many times, there were interruptions with her personal privacy with questions from a nurse. That's where we came in. Even though Dad had a nurse taking care of him, we always made sure one of us was there just to make sure things ran right so mom could have a little personal time.

There was no doubt what she was going through was difficult. At times, it must have made her feel like she was a prisoner also, trapped in her own home. Her stress level was getting worse. Even though we tried to do our best to make her life easier, our concerns were for Dad. The way we justified it, he was helpless, and mom, well, she still had her life intact and could take care of herself.

We soon found out how wrong we were. She needed our help too, not physically but mentally. She started to rely on her drinking more for mental release. In our eyes, it was better than being on tranquilizers or drugs; at least she was able to assist the nurses when needed. It never got out of control, so who were we to tell her to stop. We figured we could handle it if it got out of control.

This disease finally took over all Dads' body. He lost the movement in his hands and his head completely. It was then when we reached the end of our rope, and felt doomed. **Now we had no means of communicating with him.**

How in the world were we going to figure out even his simplest needs, like the urgency to use a bedpan? He could not relay that need to us anymore. Thank goodness, mom and Dad had this mental telepathy communication throughout their married life, at least she did, which used to amuse him. She could always tell what was on Dad's mind. Most of the time he made jokes about it, now it came in handy. She seemed to be able to look into his eyes and ask a question and for some unexplainable reason sensed what he needed. For a while it was working, at least there was no major problems to complicate his health. **We got lucky!**

Just like everything else with Dad's progression, it did get harder for mom to keep guessing. I think that is when I felt Dad did not want to be bothered any more; I think he was done with everything.

I know everyone was frightened without the lack of communication. The tension in the house was becoming very strained causing more chaos and panic especially not knowing how we were going to handle his new situation.

As I think about this now here was a man who could not move one muscle in his body, all he had left was watching the TV just to kill time. Lying in bed day and night with his only enjoyment now was hearing and seeing his family. What kind of quality of life was that? Without the proper communication, we were lost. We did not know what else we could do for him. Our hands were tied.

One thing we promised ourselves especially if Dad could not communicate with us anymore, we would never give up talking to him as if he could answer us back. Never did we want him to feel we were ignoring him.

Our demand was even stronger with the nurses. Never did we want the nurses to ignore him just because he could not respond to them. We wanted them to be on their toes at all times and to treat Dad as if he was aware of what was going on. Although, that it was something we didn't know for sure ourselves since he couldn't communicate anymore.

I remember one incident we had with a nurse that made me want to scream I was so upset. It was about 9:00 in the evening and I was at my own home. For some reason I had a feeling that I needed to go over to their house. Going their that late for me was unusual since I'm always in bed by 9:30. As I pulled in the driveway, I saw the night nurse's car parked there. I was relieved because I knew that wasn't my worry a nurse did show up. Nevertheless, I still could not shake the feeling I needed to go into the house. When I walked in the door, there was the nurse sound asleep in a chair. How long I do not know. She must have figured all the hard work was finished during the day so she did not have much to do for Dad. As I rushed over to Dad's bed to check on him **I blew up** when I realized he was not getting enough air. Trying to remain calm, my hands were shaking so bad it was hard not to panic. The pressure air gauge on the ventilator was showing a problem. When that happens it usually means Dad was not receiving the proper airflow and needed suctioning, in other words he was gasping for air.

That's when I lost it, after I made sure Dad was okay I yelled at the nurse waking her up and immediately let her have it. "What in the hell do you think you're doing? My Dad's air pressure was dangerously low." Of course, the yelling caused mom to come running out of her bedroom in a panic yelling "Pam, what's wrong, why are you here?"

Unfortunately, there was never an alarm on the pressure gauge when his air supply was low. The alarm only triggered when the ventilator was not producing any air. That is why it was important to monitor him all the time especially since he could not communicate to us any more. However, that is impossible to do when your eyes are closed isn't it!

When we got Dad comfortable again, I fired the nurse. I was so furious. You know it is no wonder poor mom always slept with one eye open at night. That night I stayed with Dad until the agency sent another nurse out. I must say they were fast in sending one. They knew they screwed up big time! As I said before losing a way to communicate with Dad changed everything!

CHAPTER 24
Finding communication for Dad

I have been told miracles do exist. I have to admit what happened to us this day made us feel it was just that. Mornings at mom and Dad's house were always very hectic. Tending to all Dads' needs definitely kept the household busy. Getting him prepared for his day was a lot of work. First on the list was making sure his bladder was relieved as you assisted him. Being totally paralyzed we had to become his hands.

Ever since the beginning of his illness, especially when he became incapacitated he hated the uncomfortable feeling of a catheter, which is a small tube that is inserted into his penis so the urgency to relive himself was automatic. However, he refused to have one. At that time, it was okay with us we knew the possibility of getting infections normally went along with that procedure so we never pushed the issue. We figured it would never be a problem because all he had to do was tell us when the urge was there. Little did we know that someday he would lose the ability to communicate with us, who knew!

Now it made our job harder because without proper communication it was necessary to keep a urinal bottle on Dad's penis all the time. Our problem was he could not tell you when it was full. Naturally, so you needed to monitor the situation so there were never any overflows causing all kinds of uncomfortable situations with more work for us.

This one morning while mom was doing her normal bathroom routine with Dad looking into his eyes asking the question "do you need to relieve yourself?" As she said under her breath, "one of these days maybe he'll answer me." When all of a sudden to her surprise she noticed Dad's eyelids blink but this time slower as if he was trying to respond to her.

You see uncontrollable twitching was one of the symptoms with this disease. With Dad's illness, his eyelids were constantly blinking like a light bulb fluttering as it starts to lose its power. Therefore, we became used to the fast blinking.

Now when I think back to that morning maybe his constant blinking was not the disease and it was his way of trying to get our attention to tell us he was in control with his eyelids movements. It is odd because it didn't seem to start until after he lost the ability to move his hands and head but we never put two and two together. I cannot imagine how frustrating it was for Dad all this time as he tried to get our attention. We always knew he was a determined man however to give up was not in his nature thank goodness.

Although it did puzzle mom when she noticed his blinking was much slower now, to her that was unusual. When she excitedly called us over to the bed and said, "look kids I think your Dad is trying to respond to me." In my mind, I was thinking yeah right!

As we all stood there staring at his eyelids looking for the blinking to slow down, I'm sure we looked very funny on his end. At first, we noticed they were not moving at all, which was very unusual because to us his blinking looked like it was uncontrolled. Mom saw the concerned look on our faces and said, "I think your father is doing that on purpose let's just see if I'm right."

Then she asked Dad to blink once and he did. He was actually controlling the movement of his eyelids. At first, we thought it was our imaginations. "Hang on" she said as she proceeded to ask him to do it again. When he did, you should have heard our screams of excitement. We felt as if we just hit the jackpot! Not only did we find another way to communicate with Dad it also reassured us that he was still mentally alert. After we found that out, we started to wonder if he could possibly blink on command. As we all stood there with anticipation, I said to everyone glancing towards Dad,

"I bet deep down inside he was finally saying to himself it's about time my family noticed." Just then, he winked at me as if to say yes Pam you are right. I excitedly yelled, "did you guys see that?" I started laughing and crying at the same time, "**Dad** just answered me." As I continued to look at him I said, "didn't you Dad." He blinked as if he gave me another wink. It was as if Dad and I were having our own private conversation. Just that little episode made my day. I felt rejuvenated and ready to face anything! **Our Dad was back!**

I am not sure if this was supposed to happen since Dad's eyelids are a muscle also. Fully knowing this disease attacks all your muscles and so far, it had not shown any mercy. Maybe this time we had a reprieve giving us some hope to hang on too.

Having a new way to communicate with him was a blessing. We realized we just overcame another hurdle with his disease only this one was huge. I knew this time it was with some help from up above. I could not help wondering if there was a guardian angle somewhere guiding us. To me there is no doubt in my mind this was a **miracle** one we truly **needed!**

Now that we had some type of communication again, we needed to perfect a system so there would never be any confusion to what his answers were. We all decided to have Dad blink once for yes and twice for no. Using this process and keeping the questions simple would help for now. What a huge relief this was for the family. Without Dad being able to communicate, everything was a guessing game. Trying to track down the problem while he was lying there panicking hoping you find it before he stops breathing all together was very stressful for him and us.

The consequences of Dad not having the proper levels of oxygen going to his brain was always a major concern. Even if you could tell he was getting air, you would never know if it was adequate. There were no warning alarms on the accuracy. Unfortunately, this situation could have gone on for awhile if there was not any communication to identify the problem faster. Nevertheless, the outcome could have lead to brain damage. I cannot express this enough, communication was so important for Dad's wellbeing. Nevertheless, it was like everything else we knew it was not going to last forever.

The computer—Dad's words again.

Knowing the new system we had for communication was not going to last long we needed to look for other options before we lost this one. I knew we did not want to go through that guessing game all over again that only ends up being dangerous for Dad.

In searching for other options, it was amazing how accidentally we came across them. I remember one morning; it was my turn to help at their house. Mom and I were sitting in the kitchen having a cup of coffee when we saw Linda's car come plowing down the driveway. That wasn't unusual with the way Linda drove but it was unusual that she was over so early. She was the second shift to help.

When she came rushing in the door with excitement in her voice waving this article she had in her hands it certainly made us wonder if she had finally flipped. She didn't even stop to say good morning to us just ran straight into the living room where Dad was with this out of control yelling to us at the same time. "Mom, Pam come in here quick. I want to read this article to Dad and I want you guys to hear it too."

Linda said she was reading the morning paper when this article caught her attention. The headline said "On the Cutting Edge of Communication for the Paraplegic." It was about a medical company in Ohio who had a computer program geared for the handicapped to communicate. She proceeded to read the article to Dad and us as her voice trembled trying to hold back the tears. "Dad" she said, "what caught my eye was this article was about a man in Ohio who also has A.L.S. and is on a ventilator also. He uses this computer to communicate." Now that really got Dads attention. You could see Dad rapidly blinking his eyelids as if he was excited about this.

Linda said, "he has this device with a "bite switch" that is placed in his mouth that enables him to run the computer. This computer has a software program with an alphabet board that you can connect to any

TV screen. While using this "bite switch" he can spell out words as if he is typing them to appear on the screen for everyone to read. What do you think Dad isn't that amazing?"

Now remember this is back in 1986 when this communication device was just getting off the ground. I really can't be sure about this but I have been told Dad was the first paraplegic patient in the state of Michigan to use this software program.

When Linda continued she said "the only thing different for you Dad is they stated this man is able to use this switch in his mouth to activate the computer which means he has active muscle movement in his mouth. I know that's impossible for you to do so we will have to look at other options."

Just then, Dad's mouth quivered a little bit as Linda caught it out of the corner of her eye. She thought to herself did he just do that? I never noticed it before feeling guilty at the same time because we should have been more aware.

In all fairness to the family, you see whenever Dad was lying down his mouth stayed closed all the time. Many times, we had to pry it open to brush his teeth. When he was sitting up the opposite would happen, his mouth dropped open. It was impossible to keep it closed. All those movements take muscles power to achieve, which he did not have any more, so we became his muscles. So we thought.

Therefore, when his mouth quivered slightly we always assumed it was the air coming from the ventilator causing his lips to vibrate. However, this time it was different. It looked like he deliberately did it right after Linda mentioned his mouth movement. Then she said with caution in her voice "Dad are you trying to tell me you're able to move your mouth to use this?" He blinked once for yes. "Are you kidding me?" She said excitedly. "We never thought you could do that." Right then it made us think about other muscles movement that was still active that we have overlooked.

As Linda decided to see if she understood him correctly, she placed a toothbrush inside his mouth and asked him to move it, it was so minute you could barely notice it. Hesitantly she had to ask him if he moved it. Again, he blinked once for yes. "Wow" she said, "maybe this switch may work out for you it's certainly worth checking out don't you agree Dad?" Then his blinking was out of control again as he was showing us how excited he was. In fact, if you put your hand on his heart you could actually feel it beating fast with excitement. We knew it wasn't from panicky either. That was enough proof for Linda she was ready to go to Ohio and check this out for herself.

Linda wrote down the name of the company in Ohio who developed this computer. For us it was a huge break because Ohio was our next-door neighbor. Living in Michigan made our quest much easier. Although I know, we would have found a way to get there even if it was on the other side of the world.

I was cautiously excited with all of this realizing there might not be enough movement in his mouth for him to activate this switch then what do we do. That did not bother Linda she figured she would cross that bridge when she got there again kudos to Sister Linda for her determination.

When she contacted the man's family in Ohio his family was eager for Linda and Terry (her husband) to come and visit and see for themselves. With excitement in their stride, off they went as we waited with pins and needles until they got back. The upbeat attitude in the house was definitely exploding.

We were glad Terry went with her he was a great help around the house for Dad especially with his creative mind. He had the ability to be very handy with just about anything he touched. When we bought this motorized wheelchair for Dad, knowing it would make it easier for us to get him around. Never thinking how awkward it was going to be because now you had to have a battery for the ventilator to make it portable, which was heavy and quit cumbersome. Moreover, carrying all his equipment he needed while someone guided the wheelchair most of the time it took two of us to help.

That is when Terry decided to design a platform, which sat on the back of Dad's wheelchair in order to carry all his equipment making our life and his easier. It worked out so well we told Terry he needed to patent the idea. His only concern was making it functional for Dad.

With Terry and his creative mind going along with Linda to Ohio was perfect. He could put his mind to work as they looked at this device just in case there was a need to tweak it for Dad. "You never know" he said, "thinking one step ahead was necessary especially with saving time." We all knew how precious that was for Dad.

Linda and Terry came back from Ohio full of excitement. They both could not believe how awesome it was to see this man use his computer. This device was so sensitive just the slightest bit of movement could activate the computer reassuring them that Dad would not have any problem using it. I know Linda was a little concerned about that.

Linda asked the A.L.S. Foundation if they would follow up and contact the company for us with hopes Dad could be a candidate to try it. To our excitement, this company was eager to come out to the house and set Dad up knowing how important this is was for him. However warning us at the same time this may not be for everyone.

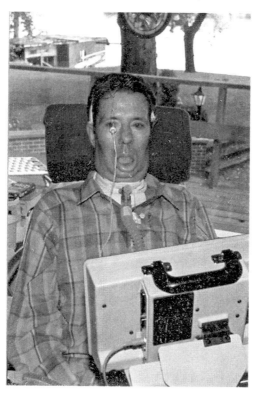

It was September 1985, which I called **C-day** meaning computer day. The Medical Company was on their way to the house. We wanted to let Dad's doctor know what was going on telling him all about this computer. We were sharing our concerns about this being a long shot especially if Dad's muscles in his mouth were too weak to move this device. It was all the convincing he needed he wanted to be at the house also. "Anyway it was time for your Dad's regular check up using that as a reason to be at the house.

Having Dad's doctor there could be beneficial for us just incase he could find other muscles movements in Dad if he did have a problem activating the switch especially with his expertise. We were impressed even someone from the A.L.S. Foundation came out also.

We paced back and forth anxiously waiting for everyone to arrive as the excitement in the house kept building. The family could not wait. For us it was as if we were getting this huge present and could not wait to open it. I could not imagine how Dad was feeling right at that moment. Thanks to Linda and Terry, we possibly could have Dad talking to us without any blinking gestures. How exciting was that!

The excitement in Dad was overwhelming you could just feel it. Being an engineer, you could vision the wheels already turning in his head. Knowing Dad I'm sure he could not wait to operate it. I bet in his engineering mind he was already trying to figure out what other muscles he could use just in case his muscles in his mouth wasn't strong enough. Too bad, it was so hard for him to communicate that to us.

Can you imagine Dad laying there trying to get someone's attention all this time feeling as if it was hopeless, getting himself all worked up inside because he knew he could show us other muscle movements. Desperately he tried to figure out a way to get his message across to us somehow. To think he was on the verge of giving up all along knowing he had a way to communicate with us made me sick inside. I told myself I couldn't go there. Looking back without any regret was the only way to keep from being depress. I kept reminding myself we had no control over all of this; we just needed to relish in the fact that we finally noticed and go on from there.

When everyone arrived at the house, I started chuckling to myself as I looked around the room. Here we had the Medical Company who was setting up all this equipment, all of Dad's medical equipment he already had, the whole family, along with the people from the A.L.S. Foundation and Dad's doctor all anxiously waiting to see what was going to happen. It was a good thing we moved Dad's bed into the living room there almost wasn't enough room for him.

Watching them set this system up was amazing. Thinking about how much technology went into this boggles your mind, of course we're still talking about 1986. This company was able to use our large TV screen to connect to the computer and with the alphabet software program that attached to the computer you could actually see it scanning the letters as they appeared on the screen when someone activated this sensor switch. I guess you could say it was the same as if the person was using their hands to type.

Only one problem we encountered the switch was so sensitive the patient using it had to have a lot of patience. Dad did struggle with it for a long time. It was at the point we figured it was not the bite switch unfortunately it was Dad having a hard time activating the switch, the muscles in his mouth was too weak.

Patiently we waited to see if anything else would work so he could activate it easier as they moved the switch around in different areas of his mouth.

We sat around talking amongst ourselves anxiously waiting to converse with Dad again. Realizing how much we missed that as we crossed our fingers at the same time hoping something was going to work. You could hear his doctor checking Dad body out all over. As he was doing his examination, he went up and down his body asking him if he could move this or that, as he tried hard to detect other muscle movements in him.

Knowing this disease affected all the muscles we never bothered to look any further. At the time, we only knew of one visible muscle movement, which were his eyelids blinking. Even though all we had was gestures with a yes or no blinking, we were still grateful for that.

Now the question was how you could take advantage of this switch with his movement of his eyelids since that was all we had to work with. As they told us unfortunately, the bite switch sensor was the only device this Medical Company had to offer for now. Even if it was possible to use the blinking of his eyelids the thought of interfering with his vision was not good. He needed to see to type out the letters.

As the doctor stood there looking at Dad wondering what to do next he detected Dad's frontal muscle moved whenever he blinked his eye. Again, we never paid attention to it.

I know this company was just about to give up on Dad with working this switch in his mouth when the doctor brought the frontal muscle to their attention. Isn't there a way to take advantage of this muscle to aviate this switch he said.

Again, you could see Dads blinking going out of control as if he was agreeing that you could do this. When I pointed this out to them saying, "Dad feels it can be done." Then explaining to them "Dad was this great engineer with a creative mind and I know he has been thinking about this muscle trying to get his point across to you right now." Looking right at Dad when I said that of course, he then blinked once for yes, which I interpreted it to this company Dad was saying yes. Well I think that was all the encouragement they needed saying "it's certainly worth trying."

As they talked among themselves "if we can find a way to attach this switch to your Dad's forehead then activating the computer should be no problem for him." Nevertheless, how can we do this?

That's when Terry spoke up and said he had this great brainstorm idea. How about using an ordinary headband, you know one you use for exercising and attach the switch wire to it. Then Dad's blinking went out of control again as if he was saying, "that's what I'm talking about." When they attached this device to the headband and placed it around Dad's forehead, it was as if Dad had a new toy. However, there were letters flying all over the screen, but as soon as they explained to Dad how to use the computer everything fell into place. It certainly did not take him long to catch on after all he was a great engineer.

Talk about our excitement now Dad had something else he could do with his time, what a blessing this was for him and the family. As he started to type out words on the screen, all our emotions went out of control. There definitely was a lot of crying going on.

It was comical how fast Dad adapted to the computer. I can still visualize the first words he typed out **"Hi Family"** as I looked over at mom she had tears running down her face. What happened to our family that day was no less than a miracle. As I thought to myself, "I think we're in trouble now" everyone started laughing.

His new toy:

It did not take Dad long before he organized his thoughts. It gave him something to look forward to in the mornings besides just watching TV. The more Dad became accustomed to the computer the more he figured mornings were his best time to activate it without getting too tired. His energy level was always lower towards the end of the day. I cannot imagine exerting energy just from blinking, but for my Dad, his body was taxed enough just from this disease.

I couldn't believe it, our family was back to having some type of normalcy again with Dad's care. At least for awhile it felt like we had a reprieve from his illness although the sounds of the ventilator were still blaring away. Nothing was going to change that.

Dad was back to being the principle decision maker in the family with his computer which was a huge burden taken off mom's shoulders. Now we had some time to get things in order.

With his new communication, we were praying there would not be any more nerve damage that could prevent him from moving his forehead. Even if we were only fooling ourselves, it felt like Dad's progression did slow down for a little while.

As he organized his finances, it seemed to occupy his time. Although, I always wondered why he wasn't as aggressive with regarding to his health. He never communicated to us about his wishes pertaining to the ventilator. He had plenty of time to voice his opinion, he never did. Not once did he mention at what point in his illness he wanted to be off the ventilator. You would have thought it was on the top of his list. I guess when you know you're facing death, it's never an easy decision to make no matter what condition you're in. At least for now, Dad was content with his life; he had something to focus on everyday. Who knew, maybe to him it was good enough.

I cannot tell you how great it was coming over to mom and Dad's house now especially in the mornings. Not only was the mood in the house more upbeat but it was awesome seeing Dad busy typing on the computer. My memories floated back to the good old days when I was a kid watching how busy he was when he brought his work home however, if you disturbed him you would have gotten into big trouble.

Dad became very efficient with the computer. If he knew who was coming over to the house ahead of time there were always messages he typed on the screen pertaining to that person, as he was ready to have a conversation with them. To me it was the best part of the day being alone with Dad and you did not have to share him with anyone else.

Since Dad's situation with his health seemed too stabilized for awhile, it was easier for mom to have some time to herself without worrying about him. She started to have sleepovers at her kids' houses. We always had a nurse at home and with Ray, it reassured her Dad's care was under control.

This one night mom decided to stay over at my house. It's funny how she told everyone it was like sleeping at a hotel. The girls loved treating her like a queen. They waited on her while she stayed in bed for most of the day as she read her books. Reading was one of mom's most enjoyable pleasures that seemed to disappear the busier she became with Dad.

That following morning before I left my house to go to hers to help, I told her to take her time and Kim would drive her home when she was ready. The reality was I did not want her back so soon. Even though there was a nurse on duty, I could not wait to have Dad all to myself. It was my special moment with him.

Dad knew it was my turn to come over so he was busy composing my message on the computer before I got there. You would be surprised how much energy and time it took as he typed one letter at a time to fill up a sentence. It's too bad he did not know how to text like everyone does today with their cell phones it would have been less work.

When I arrived at their house, the nurse was still busy finishing up with Dad's morning bathroom routine, so I patiently waited. Like a little kid, I could not wait to peek into the living room to see what he wrote to me. I wanted to go into there right away to read my message from Dad, but I realized he could not share that moment with me until the nurse was done with her morning routine. Anxiously, I waited. Whenever any of us girls were over to help relieve the nurse, they had the chance to take a break. Dad was never alone.

Finally, when I went into the living room there was a printed message on the screen for me. It was as if we were actually conversing together. Dad asked how the girls were doing. He asked if Kim liked college. Of course, asking how Jimbo was doing at work, which was his nickname he gave Jim a long time ago. He asked if he made the decision to take the other job yet, to me that was a special comment because Dad and Jim always shared conversations about work all the time. It was something they always had in common when Jim was still working at Ford Motor. Jim's job was in purchasing and Dad's of course was engineering. Jim would buy the parts and Dad would make the cars. What a combination they made and they both did a great job.

When I answered him back, it felt great. It gave me the feeling I was just shooting the breeze with my Dad just as we used to do. Sadly, as I released a big sigh I realized how much I missed that relationship.

If I closed my eyes, I could actually vision Dad in his healthier days talking with me again. Now his voice was the tapping of the keys on the computer. However, I still relished in the moment.

I remember my sister Mary telling me about her personal messages which she could not wait to see either. Her voice started to crack as she tried to hold back her tears telling me what happened. "One morning" she said, "when she walked into the living room her message on the computer said, "good morning Mary I love you." She said right away she lost it and started crying.

Of course, it did not take much for Mary to get emotional. We use to tease her and mom about their emotions all the time. They both even cried at birthday parties. Ray used to tease them by saying, "here they go again, "man the buckets," as they both stood there crying always using that phrase as he referred to all the water coming from their tears causing a flood. Then she told me there was a lot of Dad's illness she blocked out but this one made a lasting memory for her that she would treasure forever "You know Pam" she said," that was the first time I ever remember Dad telling me he loved me."

My Dad was a man who loved his children but he never was one to be verbal with his affections. His way of showing his love was by making sure his family had the best life he could give them. His affection to us was a smile, a hardy laugh at something we did, sometimes even a twinkle in his eye from laughing so hard. However, to come up to you and give you a hug and a kiss, well that never happened unless you instigated it first.

I have certainly learned from that experience. Realizing how important it is to say, "I love you" and to give hugs and kisses all the time to my children. Even now with them being adults, it is still important. We all need that affection. **Now with having grandchildren I cannot express my love enough!**

Not only was Dad good at communicate with us he also related his feelings about the nurses, **many times!** If there was something, a nurse did to him during the night that he did not approve of or it was painful. Since the night shift wasn't monitor often by us, he let everyone know with a message on the screen the next morning. This became dangerous because he was the one in control now. They had to stay on their toes constantly. Believe me if they did not he would have never given them a second chance. It was something Dad never lost when he was a boss. After a couple of times, we had to remind him that nurses were hard to come by; we could not be too fussy.

CHAPTER 25
My inspirational memory—The dove

Regrettably, not only was Dad's eye blinking getting weaker which was controlling the movement of his frontal muscle, only caused it to slow down also. It is no wonder we were so excited to see a message on the screen from him whenever we came over. We never knew if it was going to be his last.

This one morning when I was over at their house, I had this experience with my Dad that turned out to be an inspirational uplifting memory for me. Although at the time, it did not become meaningful until many years after my parents death.

You could say it was like having a psychic experience that seems to recur for me when the need is there to give me comfort. Always reminding me my parents are with me even after 22 years.

This is how it all transpired. As I stood in their living room gazing out the window this huge grayish bird flew onto their deck. I never noticed that type of a bird before. To be honest with you the only bird I ever recognized in the past was a robin even as a child. I think the reason was everyone related it to spring coming. Living in Michigan with the winters the robin was a sight to celebrate.

Anyway, as I made a remark aloud "what in the world is the name of that bird? I can't believe how huge it is." Never thinking my Dad was paying any attention to me, or even if he knew the answer. I was only making small talk trying to find something to say.

All of a sudden, I heard the noise of the computer going. When I turned around to see what Dad was typing, I noticed he had spelled out the word **DOVE** on the screen. To my surprise I said, "are you kidding me Dad is that the name of that bird how did you know that?" For some unexplainable reason, which you will find out later in this chapter that bird became a symbolic supernatural comforting image to me, which embedded in my memory forever.

When I told Dad, I was impressed he knew the name of that bird, thinking to myself well he does have a lot of idle time on his hands now to notice things like that so I'm sure he was right. Regrettable how sad it was that he never seemed to have found the time before, his life was always going 100 miles an hour.

Then I remember an old saying that popped into my mind "always take time to smell the roses." Realizing how ironic it was that it took his illness to give him the time to finally do just that. I know it taught me a life lesson. Never realizing what that day was going to mean to me later on in my life, it just remained a shadow in my memory.

It was only a year after that episode when both my parents passed away. I was hurting inside for a very long time. Even though my wonderful husband and my beautiful daughters were there for me, it still was very hard for me to get over their death.

I sometimes wonder if the reason was the illness they both suffered from. Mom dying of cancer and Dad having A.L.S. that wore on me. On the other hand, maybe the fact I lost them only nine months apart both at a young age of 62. To be honest with you I did not know the answer. The only thing I knew for sure was my heart had a huge void. The reality was my life went on and yes very happily but in my heart there was still sadness.

It was amazing after this experience I'm about to share with you looking back to that moment everything finally started to make sense to me.

There it was, this symbolic supernatural figure, which embedded in my memory, the dove, coming back to me giving me comfort and inner peace, as if I was having this spiritual psychic experience. Truly making a believer out of me knowing your loved ones spirits live on. That symbol of the dove helped me mend my heart many times throughout the years especially when another loss of a loved one from A.L.S. was so hard to take.

This started to happen to me about 10 years after my parent's death. Jim and I built the house of our dreams on a beautiful lake. Right away, it brought back fond memories of my parents' home on their lake.

Standing in my living enjoying the beautiful view all kinds of mixed emotions started going through my mind. As I stood there, feeling depressed because mom and Dad were not here to enjoy this moment with us, and feeling proud at the same time of our accomplishment, I fell into a trance gazing out the window.

An overwhelming feeling of sadness came over me, knowing how much they were missing out with their kids and our kids as they traveled down life's path without them. Trying hard to fight back the tears so my family would not notice I was crying for they would have wondered what was going on with me.

All of a sudden, these two beautiful huge grayish doves flew onto the railing of my deck. As I stood there watching them they flew under my deck into a nest they were building. Just then, this sensation of inner peace came over me. I was overwhelmed with emotion I could not explain. Never did I notice any doves flying by my home before let alone building a nest under my deck.

As my thoughts took me back to that morning I shared with my Dad just for one second I wondered could this be some type of a message from him do I dare believe that? Then reality set in; as I thought okay Pam don't be so foolish it was only my wishful thinking.

Although I have to tell you on the days when I became depressed again thinking about my parents' out came these two doves from under my deck to perch on my window looking in as if they were trying to get my attention as they sensed my sadness. When they started cooing it was as if they were telling me they were here for me. What was strange to me this went on for about a couple of years. **I guess they felt I still needed comforting.**

I knew deep down in my heart they were the spirits of my mom and dad and it was not a figment of my imagination. Maybe that is why I never said anything to anyone for a long time fearing everyone would have thought I was **CRAZY**. I just kept it my comforting secret, which seemed to work for me.

Then about seven years later, we decided to move and build another beautiful home on a golf course. Again, memories came pouring back of my parents' home. You see, even though the backside of their home was facing the lake, the front was facing a golf course. It was odd how much similarity we had with them and it was never planned it just happened that way.

As we built another deck on to our new home, I was in shock to see two doves building a nest under my deck again. Frantically thinking to myself is something going to happen to me that I am not aware of, feeling that I would need comforting again. At that point, I thought this is strange. I was positive they were following me for some bizarre reason. I was so possessed with the doves it even got to the point I would not let Jim knock down their nest even though they made a mess on my patio.

It was then I confided in Jim about my feelings. Of course, he had this grin on his face thinking I had just "flipped." There was no way my story was going to make a believer out of him although he did have his moments. Therefore, for my sake he did not touch their nest.

When I told the girls my story, they just made a joke out of it. Although when they were over, they always made a point of saying hi grandma and grandpa to the doves, especially Kimberly. Subconsciously, I think they wanted to believe it.

A year went by as I thought their meaning began to fade. For some reason they were still coming back. However, I felt my heart had mended. I figured these doves or their symbol knew their job was done. I was finally at peace with my parents' death—**so I thought,—** until the day when my youngest daughter was married. I guess they knew!

Now this will make a believer out of anyone. I had made it through my oldest daughter's wedding, which was a wonderful occasion without any sad thoughts of my parents not watching her walk down the aisle. Then making it through my first grandchild being born without them was also very tough but I made it.

However, the year my youngest Daughter Kristie, was married for some reason I became very emotional. My parents' memories became so vivid to me that day that I just couldn't get them out of my mind. It was a feeling I will never be able to explain. However, thank goodness it was the same feeling a guest at Kristie's wedding also had which blew my mind when she confined in me, at least I wasn't going crazy.

Kristie had this beautiful outside wedding. Kim and her husband Mike and little Josh, my grandson was all in it. Josh was only two and was the ring boy but we were fearful he would not make it down the aisle. Therefore, my little nephew Addy who was four pulled Josh down the aisle in this decorated wagon.

I was sad knowing how much enjoyment mom and dad would have had seeing all of this especially with all my siblings and their families there. Subconsciously they were on my mind a lot that day but I tried to keep myself busy. I knew I had to focus on being the mother of the bride.

The music began to play as Addy started pulling this wagon down the aisle with little Josh in it holding tightly to the ring pillow. As Josh got out of the wagon and turned, he saw all the people sitting there and became frightened. Hurriedly he ran into my arms quickly putting his head down on my shoulder figuring no one could see him.

With the music playing, everyone stood up to watch my beautiful daughter walk down the aisle. **All of a sudden, I felt a calming spiritual feeling surrounding me as if I just received a big hug**. As I turned to see who was hugging me no one was there, everyone was busy watching Kristie come down the isle. Never in my whole life did I ever experience something like that before.

Then when Kristie and Brian said their "I do's" I heard the cooing of doves as if they were **saying yeah!!!!!** As I glanced up into the trees, I saw **two** doves sitting on the branches looking down at this gazebo as if they were watching Kristie and Brian. In my heart I knew they were the spirits of mom and dad.

With tears in my eyes I looked around to see if anyone else had noticed it, of course no one did how foolish of me to even think that. I wanted so badly to share that moment with everyone but felt my family would have thought I was having a mental breakdown. Okay, saying to myself, I will justify this as only my desire for mom and dad to be here and it was all my imagination and let it go.

Until later at the reception, a lady whom I never met before which I found out later was a guest of one of Brian's family members, came up to me and introduced herself.

At first she complimented me on the beautiful ceremony which I thought how nice of her. Then she hesitated for a second as if she had something to tell me but didn't know where to start. My first thought was okay now what is wrong. "Pam," she said, "I don't mean to upset you but did you by some chance lose someone very close to you recently?" I looked at her with this shocking look on my face and thought what a thing to say to me on this happy occasion making me sad all over again. Furthermore, it was none of her business. I think she knew I was a little upset. When she continued she said, "please don't take this wrong but I truly feel you should know this." Still in a state of disbelief, I just stood there with my mouth open hoping someone would come and rescue me. I certainly did not want an episode like this to spoil my daughter's wedding day.

Then when I heard her say this, it blew my mind! "Pam," she said," I felt this very strong spiritual presence at the wedding today. I don't know if you believe in life the after death but I do," as she claimed she was clairvoyant. "She said, there was this presence of two spirits who were looking down at your daughter just when she said her I do's. As I looked up into the trees I saw these two doves sitting on this branch right above your daughter's head cooing."

Can you imagine how I felt right at that moment standing there with this numbness all over my body not believing what I was hearing yet feeling like I was having this out of body experience. My heart was beating so fast I thought I was going to pass out. Okay I thought either this woman is nuts or she can read my mind knowing I was feeling the same way.

This was a person whom I never met before. For her to feel my loss and my sadness of their death was unreal. Then if that was not enough for her to have the very **same spiritual, experience** that I did was overwhelming. Furthermore, she could have said one spirit instead of two. In my mind, I could have gone on and on I was so excited.

Of course, she had no idea how happy she just made me feel as I started to cry uncontrollably hugging her and saying while shaking in dismay **"yes I lost my mom and Dad."** Then she looked me right in the eyes with this big smile on her face and said, **"Pam, they were here."** Nevertheless, she left me in such a state of shock with happiness bubbling all over me I could hardly contain myself.

When I told my family about my experience, it became the main conversation at the wedding. Deep down inside I knew mom and Dad were not going to miss this special occasion. It wasn't my imagination after all, **THEY WERE HERE**!

To this day, I still have this nest under my porch and I will never knock it down in hopes they will come back every year. Although what's strange, they only seem to come back when they sense sadness in my life again.

When I lost my sister Sue to A.L.S., they were there for me. Every time another sibling died, the doves gave me comfort helping me to get through.

You know if it were not for that special moment I shared with my Dad that day, I would have never known how meaningful the symbol of the dove meant to me.

I was truly grateful for that moment. Even at the stage my Dad was in with his A.L.S., he was still able to communicate to me a true and meaningful memory that will last me a lifetime. Although, I'm sure at the time he did not realize how memorable it was going to be for me,—**OR DID HE?**

CHAPTER 26
Anniversary planning

This one morning Dad spelled out the words anniversary on the computer. "Yes" I said to him, "I know your anniversary is coming soon." He made a point of telling us it was a special year to him. Now here was a man in his condition thinking about mom and their anniversary how special was that. They were married in September 1946; now being 1986 made it a special 40th year.

I told Dad all of us kids were thinking the same way before he became ill only the 50th year was on our minds. I had to laugh to myself when I told him why their anniversary date always was easy for me to remember. Teasingly I said I was born four days later, as he typed **ONE** year and four days later with an exclamation point after the one. I got the message when I saw the big exclamation point. "You know I am only kidding," I said. Then he typed back "you were here fast enough" winking his eye at me.

As we continued to talk about their anniversary party deep down inside I was glad we were doing it this year. Not knowing what was ahead of us, wouldn't it be ironic if they both did not make it to their 40th year. I guess you never know when your highway of life will end. Make plans for the day and hope there is a tomorrow!

We did not have much time to plan their anniversary since it was only three weeks away. I do remember Dad saying before he became ill he wanted to do something special for mom this year. I can't tell you how impressed I was he was still thinking about doing that. How unselfish was that thinking about mom, it made me realize how much he really loved her. "Wow I told him that's great." "We will keep it very small." He typed **Okay.** I was glad to see he still wanted to be with people and was not embarrassed about his condition.

In a way, he was actually planning this party and we were just doing the legwork, what a good feeling it was. As we firmed up the plans I said to him "do you want to just have a few relatives and close friends?" Of course, there was a big **yes** on the computer. I could not help having a big smile on my face as we continued with the rest of the plans. He started typing more about the party as he put strong emphasis on making sure it was a surprise for mom. This made me feel great knowing all of this was really just for her.

Then he proceeded to type out his wants pertaining to his personal needs on that day. For instance, making sure he was sitting in his motorized wheelchair, before the guests came so he could feel like he was welcoming the guests. I thought what an amazing attitude to have. He also wanted to make sure we kept a close eye on him just in case he looked too tired. Then without interrupting the party, we could help him back in bed. Again, what a great reason for having his bed in the living room even when he was lying down it still made him feel like part of the crowd. "Dad" as I reminded him, "you don't have to worry with all your girls around."

As we finished the plans before mom came home, he typed **"ring"** on the computer. "Dad do you want us girls to buy mom a ring?" "Yes" he typed. At that point, I almost lost it, as my eyes became watery trying to hold back my tears. My Dad was a remarkable man. I was amazed with everything he was going through with his illness it was still important to him to make mom happy.

When I told the girls, what he wanted us to do I had tears in my eyes all over again knowing this probably was their last anniversary together. In a way, it was nice to have something to celebrate in their house again. It gave the house life and made you feel like nothing had ever changed.

He knew having us girls shop for him we would make sure we did a lot of price comparing before we chose the right gift even though it was his money. Boy did we have a lot of fun spending it!

In Dad's healthier days us girls always shopped for him he either trusted our judgment or really didn't want to take the time to do it himself. Just like any other man, if he shopped at all it was always the day before the event. Having us doing it for him, he never had to worry, especially if it might have forgotten. He was always thinking ahead, I think that was very smart. I have to say the best part with walking into a jewelry store and being girls was feeling like we could buy anything. When we got home and showed Dad the ring that it had mom's birthstone in it, he was very pleased. On the computer he typed, "I **knew you girls could do it, thanks.**"

Trying to keep the secret from mom along with hoping we did not have any health complications with Dad before the party made us all nervous. You never knew from day to day how he was going to feel, it certainly kept us anxious.

I couldn't believe how the whole attitude in the house was contagious, everyone was going around bubbly and happy. Although mom did not realize what was going on, although she was a little suspicious of the uplifting attitude. When Dad first became ill, I thought we would never see another family party in their house ever again. I am glad I was wrong we needed that boost.

It was funny we had no problems getting mom out of the house so we could decorate and set things up. All we had to say was, "mom, I think you need to take a trip to the grocery store" and she was out the door. Everyone knew mom's trips to the grocery store were not short ones, it was her time to socialize and she enjoyed that.

One of our biggest concerns with keeping this a surprise from mom was the panic she would have had seeing all the cars parked in the driveway, when she came home from the grocery store, thinking something happened to Dad. Therefore, we decided to tell her as soon as we came down her street that we were having a party at her house. The funny thing was it never registered it was for her anniversary she didn't give it a second thought. With everything mom had gone through with Dad's illness I am sure, she just lost track of time. Everyday just became another day nothing changed for her.

We kept Dad's wishes and had him sitting in his chair to welcome the guests as they arrived. I will never forget the looks on their faces when they first saw him. Some of them had not seen Dad since he was on the ventilator. They had no idea what to expect. We even warned them in the invitation but still it did not make it easy for them. It was hard for us to break the tension of everyone being uncomfortable until we saw mom pull into the driveway then the festivities started.

Everyone was excited for mom. When she came in the house and turned into the living room everyone yelled **SURPRISE.** It threw her for a loop. Still it did not register why everyone was there. She looked very confused until she really noticed all her friends and family. Then it was "man the buckets again" good old Ray teasing her about her crying again. It was so special when I looked over towards Dad; just for a second I thought I saw a little twinkle in his eye. I know if he could have smiled, it would have been from ear to ear with pride.

Standing there looking around the room at all their friends and relatives I could not help notice the sadness on their faces as they looked at Dad. It was still hard for us to adjust to his illness and we were around him all the time.

When everyone was finished eating we gave mom her gift from Dad. When we told her he communicated to us that he wanted to buy this for you, there was not a dry eye in the house when she opened it. I know the party truly caught mom off guard. Although it was, wonderful seeing her enjoy herself again. It was the first time since Dad's illness she could relax and enjoyed her friends and family.

The day was amazing it could not have been any nicer. It was so warm and beautiful outside we were able to get Dad out of the house for a little while. For a second I pretended like life was back to normal again and we were back to having Sunday dinners. Wiping the tears from my eyes, I realized how much I truly missed those times. Sadly, they were gone forever. Even though everyone enjoyed that day we still had to be careful not to have any embarrassing moments for Dad like an accident with his bathroom needs. Whenever he was away from his computer, it was hard for him to communicate to us about his personal needs. While we had a nurse around to help take care of Dad, all of his girls still hovered over him like hawks making sure there were no accidents. After all, we made Dad a promise he would never have the feeling of being embarrassed, especially in front of all his friends and relatives. It was hard enough for him as it was. This was the main reason why we kept the guest list small. It was important to us to make everyone feel comfortable with his situation and he had confidence in us that we would take care of him.

In the end, it became the boost mom needed. Her beautiful smile was from ear-to-ear again. It's too bad we could not have stopped time and bottled that special moment. Later on when Dad's illness became worse, we could have used the extra boost. Throughout his illness, we never knew where his life's path was going to lead us. After awhile we learned to go with the flow. If you did not it would tear you apart. That day we embraced every moment we had left with Dad and we never looked back.

CHAPTER 27

Friends dealing with Dad's illness and physical changes

My Dad was always a handsome man even in his later years he never lost his good looks. He was one of the lucky people who were fortunate to keep his youthfulness. I fondly remember this funny story, which pertained to Dad and his handsome looks.

When I was only 16 and started working, I didn't have a drivers' license so Dad took me back and forth everywhere. This one evening when he came to pick me up one of the older women I worked with knew he was coming. As she glanced towards his car and immediately took a second look she said, "Pam is that you're boy friend out there waiting for you? I thought your Dad was coming." I laughed and said, "are you kidding that is my Dad." She responded, "it is! Wow he's good looking is he married," she said jokingly. I just looked at her oddly; as I thought to myself, you must be kidding. First, why in the world would she be looking at my Dad in that way what is wrong with her? He's my Dad.

I never did say anything to Dad about it, because I thought he would have been embarrassed. Of course, now many years later with myself being much older, I realized it was a huge compliment to give anyone in his or her later years.

When I was a teenager, I was proud to tell everyone he was my Dad. Never did I mind him taking me places. I think that's why I took the changes to his appearances from his illness so hard. If it were not for his disease and the way, it took over his body features he would have just aged handsomely. I know it never bothered Dad he was not a vain man. It was just my feelings.

You see with this disease Dad's facial appearance changed tremendously because the muscles in his face died. It was noticeable when Dad was sitting up; the force of gravity took over his skin pulling on his facial muscles causing them to droop. When the muscle died in his face, which was from the disease, everything would just hang, consequently even his jaw, causing his mouth to stay open all the time. It was as if he lost a lot of weight and had a lot of excess skin, although you knew it was atrophy of the muscles. There was nothing to prevent this from happening. Under that frozen facial expression, he was still our handsome Dad. I always tried to avoid him seeing his reflection when he was sitting up, I was worried it would make him feel self-conscious about the way he looked and would not want to sit up any more. To lie in bed all the time without moving could have caused all kinds of complications to his health. Pneumonia could set in his lungs; he could get bedsores from too much pressure on one area of his body. Hence, the need to keep him moving was important.

I know it bothered the little grandkids when they saw this frozen expression on his face. I could see it in their reactions. Dad did not look like the grandpa they once knew. Unfortunately, they became frightened to be close to him. Whenever the little ones were around when I was over I always made sure he was lying down so that didn't happen.

Then there were times we had to be cautious when he was sitting up not to put too much pressure on his bladder. It was always a constant battle of being on our toes.

Nevertheless, as he progressed with his disease things did become more complicated. The only way we could deal with it was take it one day at a time. Believe me even though the going got tougher we never gave up. We still had our Dad with us and **YES,** that was a blessing in our eyes.

When Dad's friends came to visit, I could feel their sorrow. I was truly grateful they came often even though it was very hard to see Dad in his condition. Our family certainly understood, there's no doubt at times it was even hard for us and we were around him everyday. At least we had somewhat of a chance to adjust as he went through the changes in his illness. I know for anyone that had not seen Dad since he was healthy it really astounded them. I'm sure it was the reason why his visitors stopped coming by as often. It was a feeling of helplessness not knowing what they could do for him. Even if they tried to make light of the situation it still made them feel uncomfortable.

Some of Dad's friends became very depressed when they went home. One friend in particular who went through high school with them tried to come over as much as possible at least for mom's sake. It was very hard for her to come into the living room and say hi to Dad. To see him in that condition truly made her sick.

She had a lot of love and respect for Dad and several times referred to him as her hero. Dad and mom were there for her when she went through a very bad divorce. They supported her throughout the whole incident and helped her get back on her feet. They were life long friends. After awhile even her visits were only with mom as she stayed in the kitchen trying her best to avoid going into the living room where Dad was. I know she felt ashamed and had a lot of guilt over that, but seeing Dad in that condition was too hard for her to handle. We always tried to reassure her keeping mom occupied was also helping Dad. We knew he understood and was grateful she was there for mom. Eventually her guilt got the best of her and her visits became less and less. The last time we saw her was at Dad's funeral even then all she could do was apologize and ask mom to forgive her. After that, we never saw her again, even when mom died.

One thing Dad truly looked forward to was the visitors from work. They would always come in small groups. I do not know if they planned it that way but it certainly made the conversation flow better. He truly enjoyed all the different conversations amongst his co-workers. Dad was always interested in what was going on at Ford Motor Company even though he was no longer working it still made him feel like he was still in the loop and involved.

I will never forget this one day when a group of Ford engineers who worked closely with him on the Taurus and Sable project came by. It was shortly after the launch of these carlines, which Dad was not able to attend because of his illness. These carlines were now in production and in the dealerships.

One engineer Malcolm, who was British, became very good friends with Dad. They worked closely together in Germany. In fact, Dad was responsible for bringing Malcolm and his young family here to the states to work for Ford Motor Company, which started their strong foundation of friendship.

That day was remarkable beautiful outside. We couldn't wait until they arrived, so we decided to take Dad out side in his wheelchair so he could be ready when they pulled in the driveway. We knew we were going to take many pictures so we wanted him ready ahead of time. When Malcolm got out of the car, he was carrying this beautiful trophy. They were going to present this trophy to Dad after the launch but unfortunately his illness got in the way and he couldn't be part of the celebrations.

You should have seen the excitement in mom's eyes. I know Dad was feeling very proud that day also. As they presented the trophy to Dad, my eyes got all teary. I could not help thinking how different all of this would have been if it were not for his disease. It really was a shame he couldn't relish in his allotment achievement.

After Dad and mom passed away, Jim and I became good friends with Malcolm and his wife June. Even to this day 22 years later we are still good friends. With Jim also working at Ford Motor Company at the time, he knew all of Dad's friends and associates, so it was easy for us to have the same friendships.

You know I have never told Malcolm this before but he never knew how much comfort he has given me throughout the years with having their friendship. Every time I was around Malcolm, we always managed to bring up Dad in our conversation. Because of their close friendship, he has always made me feel like my Dad was still around. I truly thank him for that comfort.

CHAPTER 28

Dad in charge as he hires our special nurse, Denise

September came and went and it was starting to get colder. It had been about two months since we started around the clock nursing care for Dad. We were finally in a better routine with the nurses. I know Dad being able to communicate now made the quality of his care more in tune to them, which made our lives easier naturally, because now he could voice his opinion.

When you think about the importance of having proper communication, it becomes an essential tool for anyone's wellbeing. The thought of Dad losing the ability to use the computer was scary. We knew it would happen eventually but for now, we just enjoyed this moment in time.

By now, we were very fortunate for the most part to see the same nurses regularly. However, we still had a few nurses that were not reliable. Mostly not showing up when their shifts started. Of course, Dad was still being finicky with the ones he did not like. Now he had his computer to help complain about them.

I remember this one nurse. She and Dad went back and forth for about two days. She signed up for the midnight shift making a comment that it was her favorite one to work. My gut feeling told me she didn't like the physical labor that went along with home care unless the shift was easy. Most of the time the midnight shifts usually went that way.

Repeatedly we reminded her Dad was the one in charge and he is aware of what is going on around him. We hoped she would be a little more in tune to his needs as we reminded her that Dad didn't hesitate to let us know if there was something he felt was wrong, hoping it would make her more aware this shift wasn't a piece of cake.

With Dad being on a ventilator, his care was more complicated. There was never any down time not even at night. Just because everyone was sleeping at midnight even Dad at times, his equipment still needed monitoring, especially the ventilator. His hose that connected to the vent and to his trachea needed cleaning often for proper airflow. That was on rule we couldn't stress enough!

One day he told us he was afraid of this nurse falling asleep on the job, which he caught her couple of times already. At first Dad did not say anything to us when it happened. Then he told us how nervous he was having her around, even to the point of being afraid something might happen to cause his death. However, he did give it two days for our sakes in the end he had enough of it. The next day on the computer there was "**NOT HER AGAIN,**" we knew what he meant.

We did not hesitate to let the agency know why we did not want her back even if it meant we were taking her place the next day. Thank goodness, we didn't need to do it for long the agency found a replacement right away. Even though we had 24 hours nursing care, we were around all day also. There were things we did for Dad also. We were the ones that took him outside when it was a beautiful day. We even took him down the street for walks in his motorize wheelchair. Can you imagine how great that felt for him, to have other views to focus on. Unfortunately, even that was a major production. All the time it took at least two of us.

Morning times for Dad were the busiest. There was so much to do just for his personal hygiene; and then on top of that, you had his equipment to keep clean, which kept you very busy. By the time afternoon came, everyone was worn out including Dad.

One thing that was sad for me to see Dad go through, was no more enjoyment from his morning showers, now they turned into sponge baths. When we were kids he loved to have us massage his head at night, especially when he had a stressful day at worked. Man did he enjoy that one. Sadly, he could no longer feel the calming sensation of running water on his head when he was having his hair washed. Now it was dry powder shampoo being comb through his hair. He was hooked up to so many tubes and wires, you couldn't take the risk of getting them wet they may have short circuit. Even brushing his teeth no longer existed that changed to just wiping out his mouth with antibiotic wash. Even that was hard for us to do, after awhile with not being able to move your muscles anymore they become stiff and harden which became impossible for us to open his mouth.

I think the biggest thing for Dad to give up with his grooming was going from a straight razor to an electric one with shaving. The potential risk of being cut was always there. Being on blood-thinning medication, we didn't need any excess bleeding.

Of course, those changes were minute compared to the whole scheme of things. Without an energized morning nurse, all of those grooming issues would be ignored.

With a midnight shift nurse, at least we girls could go home at night to our own beds and not worry about Dad, especially with Ray living with them. However, we all felt it was very important never to leave mom alone, after all, we were the ones that insisted on having home nursing care for Dad instead of going to a nursing home.

Of course, mom's sleeping at night for her didn't matter, it was not quality rest. She always slept with one eye open all the time anyway, no matter how secured things were. Ray on the other hand never had any problem sleeping. Most of the time mom had to wake him up if something was wrong with Dad, although it was still comforting to mom to have him there with her.

I know it was tough on mom having strangers coming in her house at all different hours. It was starting to wear on her. Whenever we were over we tried to make sure she took a nap during the day so she could catch up on her rest, at least she felt comfortable knowing we were there supervising.

Even though we were very fortunate with the quality of care Dad was receiving from the nurses, it still did not take the stress away from mom. I truly think she would not be stress free no matter where Dad was. In our eyes, we justified the situation with at least he was taken care of in his own home.

With the quality of care he was receiving, I'm proud to say every time he saw different doctor they were very impressed to see him in such good condition, especially with being immobile. We always knew we were taking excellent care of Dad however; to have a health professional make that comment made us feel good. It was a great compliment to our family and to the nurses caring for him. Nevertheless, as nice as it was we would have not had it any other way. He was our Dad and we took pride in caring for him. Even though we knew his disease would get worse, the reality was we would have done anything for our **Dad!**

With all the different nurses, coming and going this particular nurse really stood out. My family will never forget her. Denise was her name and boy did her and Dad click right from the start. She was young and single so she had no balancing act between work and home life, which worked out in our favor.

Whenever we needed her, she was there for us. To this day, I do not know how she arranged that with the agency, knowing they had the last say where you worked. Who were we to question that, we were grateful it worked out as well as it did.

I sometimes wondered if meeting my brother Ron helped in her decision. I remember the first time she saw him; her attraction for Ron was obvious with the family. Even though he was living on his own, he came around mom and Dad's house often to visit. Ron was single, had a great job working at Ford Motor Company, and drop dead handsome what a catch for anyone lady, however it turned out to be only a infatuation.

With all the nurses, caring for Dad there was no doubt he felt the most secure with Denise. They had this special bond right from the start. She always spoke very highly about him and always treated him as if he was her Dad too. This always impressed me.

Not only was she this skilled nurse but she became a friend to our family as well. It was reassuring for us to have that combination. I'm sure a situation like that don't happen often in the home care business.

There were times when mom needed a nurse because one did not show up, all she had to do was call Denise and she was right there. That just proved how much she cared for our family.

I know as a professional it's hard to have your emotions involved with your patient. Always you had to react with your mind and not let your heart be involved.

The connection between Denise and Dad was amazing. I always used to laugh about all the conversations Dad and Denise had. She never let it bother her that Dad was communicating on a computer. She would be busy tending to his needs and constantly talking to him at the same time as if they were conversing back and forth in a conversation. It was funny to peak in the living room and watch. You could see Dad trying to type back his comments to her on the computer, but before he was even finished, Denise would already be starting on another conversational topic, as if she already knew what he was going to say. I know if Dad could have moved his eyes freely, I can see him right now as he tried to keep up with their conversation making this gesture of rolling his eyes, as if to say to Denise "aren't you done talking yet?" At least he never got bored when she was around. It was amazing how comfortable she felt being around Dad. Never did she let his handicap bother her. Today when I think about their relationship it still brings tears to my eyes how meaningful it was.

After Denise was working for us for awhile she made this comment about our family that made us beam with pride. She said, "how overwhelming it was to see our devotion and dedication we had for Dad. Throughout her career, I know she met many different families with all kinds of illnesses. Therefore, we felt it was special for her to say that to us. She felt very comfortable with our family. I remember her making a comment one day wishing Dad was her only patient. Believe me Dad didn't let that comment slip by him. I know he was already planning on Denise's future with us. Not only did she take excellent care of him she was also good for his self esteem always reminding Dad he still had a lot of quality of life he could still look forward to even with his disability.

We used to tell her the story about Dad buying two condominiums in Florida that he was hoping to use when he retired. Now how sad it was he could never go there again. That's when a light bulb went off in Denise's head as she started to plant this bug in Dads ear. I'm sure she was the one that convinced Dad it still was not too late to do that. She shared with him ways that they could make it happen; of course, she was speaking from experience. I know she took a couple of journeys with patients before while caring for them. I think at one at one point in her career she was a private nurse before she went to work for the agency. Again, Dad took note of that.

CHAPTER 29
The Florida trip, Dad's last

It totally surprised us one morning when Dad came up with this great idea, although we all knew who was behind it. When he started typing the word Florida on the screen, we didn't understand what he was trying to tell us. I thought he was making a comment about the condominiums in Florida, asking if they were doing okay? Then when he typed, "how hard do you think it would be for me to take a trip down to Florida one more time?" That comment blew my mind. For a minute, I thought the disease went to his brain thinking he was going crazy.

Then he proceeded to type rent a motor home. When I looked at the screen I could not believe he was saying that either. "Dad, what in the world are you thinking? Are you trying to say rent a motor home and drive down to Florida?" When he typed "yes," I was amazed that in his condition he was even thinking about do something like that. I was so baffled all I could say was why would you want to take that risk?

Well that's when Linda came into the room asking what is going on. That all Dad needed to get her attention. She said, wow I think that's a great idea, **NATURALLY!** "You know when you think about this, it can be possible with all his equipment being portable. The ventilator does have a portable battery so maybe it's not a crazy idea after all."

Then you saw a big "**YES**" on the screen as if to say to Linda that's exactly what I mean. Of course, Linda went on to say, "we can't take the risk of doing this by ourselves it's impossible, we would need a nurse to come with us." When he typed, "Denise" on the computer it was then we knew who was behind all of this planning,

"the cat was out of the bag.". "What a great idea," Linda said "maybe we can convince Denise to take a leave of absence or a long vacation from her work to help us." Well, you could have guessed what Dad typed back, **GREAT IDEA!** It was comical how this was planned without us realizing it.

Now Linda was on a role with the planning. "If Denise goes she said, "we need to compensate her for working for us because it wouldn't be a vacation for her." Again Dad typed I am sure she is aware of that. As we all stood there thinking about the possibilities Linda said, "you know maybe I can go too, but I would have to bring Ryan," who was only four and not in school yet. Naturally Dad typed, **YES,** as if to say, "what another great idea," knowing she was going to say that anyway.

Now Linda was unstoppable as her ideas kept flowing. "I'm sure we can convince Ron to go also, he can drive the motor home. If we have any mechanical problems on the trip down he can fix them." You could probably guess he was in total agreement with that also. Dad knew what he was doing planting the idea in Linda's head, as she went on and on while Dad was agreeing with her, as if their heads were together planning everything by themselves.

We all knew having Ron go was very important. He was the only one in the family who had a mechanical knack with anything. Since his work was on change over and everyone had to take mandatory time off it worked out great for everyone. It was looking like everything was falling into place, **AMAZINGLY!**

For mom, I know she was a little apprehensive about the trip but with Denise going made all the difference in the world with reassuring her. She could actually relax and enjoy herself again.

Just think for Dad to see the ocean view one more time would be worth all the hassle everyone would go through to bring him there. I have to say most of us thought Dad was crazy about all of this but my sister Linda was determined that it was going to work out. **What else was new with her!**

If it wasn't for Denise reassuring us she had done this before, even though her patient was not in Dad's condition although, in a wheelchair. Helped to give us the confidence we needed. She was very careful in telling her work she was taking a planned vacation. Never did she mention she was going to be taking care of a patient while she was gone. It was her own time so I'm sure there wasn't any concerns. Who knows if this all worked out maybe she would be tempted to stay longer in Florida choosing to take some personal time as well. I'm sure Dad wouldn't have mind.

Once everything was confirmed, it was Linda's job to find a big enough motor home that could accommodate a wheelchair and all of Dad's equipment. I figured that was going to be the hardest task to do. To my surprise, I was wrong, she found one. Now everything was in place and ready to go. I still could not believe they were going to do this. They never had one roadblock, which was very unusual. I have always wondered that maybe this trip was meant to be.

The day they left, I had so many mixed emotions watching them pack the motor home. Everyone was excited but a little apprehensive at the same time although, ready to go. Here was Ron, Linda, little Ryan, mom and Denise, and Dad packed and ready to go. Of course, you could not forget Ray he was not going to miss out on the fun, after all he's done for Dad, he needed a break too.

When Denise organized the motor home it looked like a traveling hospital, not once was she apprehensive she really knew her stuff. As I sadly watched them pull away that morning, standing in their driveway, I could not help wondering if this was the last time, I was going to see my Dad alive. I quickly tried to think of something else before I started crying. I had to feel happy for him seeing Florida one more time, fully knowing this was going to be his last time. He truly enjoyed the sounds of the ocean and the walks on the beach. However, this time his walks became wheelchair rides. Still with his illness to be able to do that was a great accomplishment. Linda reassured me they were going to take walks on the beach no matter how difficult it was going to be. Sadly, their trip was not only Dads last time to see the ocean unfortunately it was mom also. However, at the time we did not know it was going to be mom's last time.

After being in Florida for two weeks, Linda needed to come home. Leaving earlier than mom and Dad was hard for her but two weeks was long enough for her to be away from her family. Since Dad was doing great and the rest of them were not ready to come home yet Linda and Ryan flew home.

Later Linda told me at first she was nervous going to Florida; however, it was something she never regretted. She was among the last ones in the family to see Dad so happy again.

It was wonderful what the trip did for mom and of course Dad's morale. Even though he physically couldn't do anything just changing his view was uplifting enough for him, especially the beautiful ocean sight. Only lasting for three weeks it was exactly "the shot in the arm" everyone needed. I felt the trip proved how much you could accomplish when you put your mind to it. I have to say looking back it was no doubt Dad knew how to live life with his disease.

I do believe that trip proved to us how well Denise fitted in with the family. Dad was never in danger with her around; she really knew her "stuff". In fact he was so impressed with her when they got back he offered her a full time job working for us. We knew Denise was ready for a change and was grateful for the chance when Dad offered it.

In a way, I was surprised she accepted because she knew working for Dad was only going to be temporary. I'm sure she felt it would not be a problem to get her old job back, she had many skilled years under her belt. We were very blessed having her by our side.

CHAPTER 30
Ron's wedding

It was 1987 and spring was in the air. Everyone was impressed how well Dad made it through the winter without any major health issues. I know we had Denise to thank for that. Not once did Dad get any type of pneumonia that seems to be common with bedridden patients. There was no doubt the quality of his care was something to brag about.

This year our family finally had something to celebrate. Ron announced he was getting married. Remember the fussy brother. Well he finally found the love of his life her name was Kim. Although, it was too bad she never had the chance to know Dad in his healthier years. Coming into a large family and having Dad ill at the same time must have been hard for her to adjust. Unfortunately, we never got the chance to know Kim very well everyone became caught up in caring for Dad. The important thing was Ron was happy and in our eyes, that counted a lot.

When Ron told Dad about the wedding Dad was determined to go. He never missed any of his children's weddings and this was not going to be any different. He insisted on going to the ceremony if nothing else, so he could see Ron say his "I do's." Dad wanted to be part of everyone's life as long as he could.

Of course getting Dad organized to do that was a lot of effort on everyone's part since all his equipment always had to go with him. It certainly was not as easy as walking out the door. Just getting Dad dressed was complicated. Always needing at least two people to help, which was something we did every morning with Dad. Just because he was bedridden not once did he stay in a hospital gown all day long just because it was easier to care for him. Getting him dressed every morning was important; it made him feel normal, and not just an invalid. We even had Dad in a suit for the wedding To this day I don't remember how we did it, but we did.

I know it must have been tough for Kim having Dad at the wedding, worrying how her guest would feel seeing him in the condition he was in. Brides always want their wedding day to be perfect. There were many pictures taken of the bridal party. Knowing Ron, he wanted his Dad to be part of them. I am sure if Dad had his computer with him so he could communicate to Ron, he would have refused to be in the pictures, especially in his condition. He knew it was going to be Ron's last memories of him and he did not want them to be sad ones.

It didn't take long for Dad to get tired and wanted to go home. Mom decided to stay for awhile and visit with the relatives. When Ray and Denise took Dad home, I felt a little sad thinking this was the first wedding of his children that he did not dance the night away. I was wondering if mom was feeling the same thing.

No sooner did I think, the music began to play. It was shortly after dinner when I saw mom's enjoyment turn into grief. The D.J. began to play the first song. How ironic was it when I heard them playing Dad's favorite song "Mac the knife," by Bobby Darin? I could not believe it when I heard it. Whenever that song played, Dad would grab mom and pull her on to the dance floor and away they went. As soon as I heard the song playing, I looked over towards mom and saw her crying. I knew right away that she was thinking of Dad. Jim asked her to dance but it was not the same all she wanted to do was go home. Even though she was having a good time, she remembered all the good times she used to have with Dad, which was very hard for me to see disappear. Reality was setting in for mom; her world as she once knew no longer existed.

It was not very long after the wedding Ron became busy with his new life. He finally had a someone new to focus on, his new wife

Kim. I know it was hard for Kim to see Dad in his condition, so Ron tried hard to shield her from all the chaos that was going on in the house especially as Dad's illness started to take a downward fall.

I do know this if Kim had had a chance to know Dad before his illness, she would have immediately gotten a big kick out of how much Ron was so much like Dad. It was uncanny how they had the same type of humor. In fact, most of us kids acquired that same trait but Ron's was more pronounced. I can even hear her right now saying to Ron "so that's who you take after."

CHAPTER 31
The family stress many breakdowns

It wasn't very long after Ron's wedding that the family was back on our roller coaster ride with our emotions. At least for a little while we had some enjoyment in our life to celebrate. Thank goodness, Ron had someone to lean on now. It certainly was not getting easier going through Dad's illness if you did not have the loving support besides the family to help you get through.

With Ron, being married, mom and Dad only had two more children left to see settled down and be happy, Sue and Ray. I know one of Dad's wishes was to see all his kids settled down and raising families of their own before he left this earth. I think that is every parent's wish. It makes you feel better knowing they will be okay without you. Unfortunately, we do not have control over that, do we? I am sure our destiny planned when we are born.

It was obvious Dad was having trouble operating the computer again. Nevertheless, we all knew this was coming but we hoped we had more time before facing this crisis again. I think for awhile we were living in a dream hoping his progression was stabilizing. It certainly made us realize reality was coming back and it was all down hill now.

His blinking movement that was controlling his frontal muscle was slowly disappearing. I think we were oblivious with everything flowing better, that it only made us panic even more when notice it was happening. We never wanted to let our guard down, nevertheless here we were. Thinking about any other options for communication just added to the tension in the house especially knowing we had to work fast. Time was never on our side!

It is no wonder everyone's stress level started to hit rock bottom. Although it was more evident with mom and Sue, unfortunately they already had mental crutches they were dealing with before Dad's illness.

When I talk about the importance for all of us to have some loving support to lean on besides the family, it never dawned on me about mom. Even though she had all of us, it was not like having your own loved one, the person whom you share your life with, holding you and telling you everything is going to be alright. The love of her life was fighting for his.

Watching Dad try harder and harder to control his blinking knowing it was the end of his communication was heart breaking. Poor Dad, either he would blink uncontrollably or there would be nothing at all. As if he had enough and said he was done. You know he had to be depressed to give up. Throughout his illness he was our rock, he gave us the strength to get through, now it was our turn to give back.

We tried to look at all the different scenarios causing him to have trouble with his blinking. Thinking his eyelids was drying out from staying open most of the time. Maybe they just needed a simple cure like liquid tears. Sadly, only to find out that was not the problem. **It was the disease doing its destruction, again.**

My stress was starting to turn into anger. All I could think of was this disease going to take over every muscle in his body? Come on give him a break! Why did it have to rob him of everything? If we cannot communicate with him anymore then what in the world can he do?

Yes, I know we had to count our blessings and be grateful Dad had some type of communication with us for a little while. Looking back, we even thought that was going to be impossible, but it happened.

Now to think about his future care with all the new possibilities of different problems compounding his health was overwhelming. His disease was progressing so rapidly it was not easy to go backwards and play the guessing game all over with his needs. Now there was not any room for error. One slip up could definitely end his life especially with his immune system being compromised even more now.

I remember in the beginning of Dad's illness the professionals saying this disease would never take over his eyes. Now I realized they meant his sight, all along I was thinking eye movement. I guess it was a good thing we did not know that ahead of time, at least we were not always holding our breath waiting for it to happen.

We had many wonderful times along this journey with Dad's illness, only proving to us how to live life with this disease as we learned to take it one day at a time. When I think about my worst day of Dad's illness, it was when I could actually feel his depression start to get the best of him. Even Denise could not get him in a good mood anymore. To be honest with you he was always giving me hope as I watched him day by day going through his illness always in a good frame of mind. **Now,** do I dare admit our family was finally up against a brick wall? I know we were feeling just like Dad, realizing the end is near.

It was hard to focus on anything else as you watched him lay there in a state of hopelessness. Just thinking of other things that could possibly happen to him now without proper communication was a frightening thought.

I could not stop my negative thoughts why God had to take everything away from him, feeling it was not fair. We always managed to overcome each hurdle we encountered, however this time we were slowly running out of options. I think for the first time we were about to give up and give in to this disease.

Mom's Physical Crutch:

With all of mom's stress, unfortunately she was finding more comfort in her drinking. We always thought she was handling it with a beer now and then. However, it was alarming to see it becoming a need as the enjoyment just flew out the window. In the past, she always put certain restrictions on herself, which to us meant control. Unless she was on vacation never would she have a beer before the afternoon. I'm sure a lot of us can relate to that. Nevertheless, that disappeared making us notice it was no longer just a problem but an addiction. You could see how obvious it was with her trying to conceal her beer long before lunchtime. It did not help either when we politely brought it to her attention.

If that was not enough, her smoking became more frequent. Even when we told her it was not helping her cough that she seemed to get around this time every year. It was as if she did not care about herself anymore. Dealing with mom's smoking was always a problem for us all our life. Many times, it caused arguments between her and Dad.

This one argument they had way before Dad became before ill was caused from him nagging her to stop. Her comment to him was always the same, "I will quit when I get cancer." At the time, she meant it to be sarcastic; sadly, it eventually became her demise. I used to wonder if making a comment like that was her way of getting our attention. No doubt, it worked for a little while. Then everyone was back to everyday life and just accepted it.

I will admit though, mom was always a polite smoker. She even had a daily routine with her smoking, which amused me. When she was at home, she would only smoke in the kitchen. She had a certain ashtray she carried everywhere she went. At the end of the day, it was cleaned and ready to use the next day. Now tell me if that was not control. I do give her a lot of respect she always was cautious about smoking around us kids. Mom was so cautious she even had a portable smoke eater that she always used to help vent out the smoke. You would have thought if she had the will power to be that concern for us, that she would have been strong enough to quit.

I can picture her right now in the corner of her kitchen with her cigarette burning in her favorite ashtray with the smoke eater on. You know, to this day I still have her favorite ashtray. I have not smoked a day in my life. However, when I take it out of the drawer and hold it makes me feel like mom is nearby. It is funny how we cherish some of our loved ones personal possessions differently. Even though it was part of her terrible habit, it was my **MOM.**

Sister Sue melts down:

While trying to deal with mom's emotions especially with everything that was going on with Dad we did not realize our little sister Sue was crashing down even more. Her emotions compounded with all different types of problems. Dad's illness was just the last straw for her.

All of this started for her about a year before Dad's illness. Sue was still living at home. For many years, she had been trying to come to terms with her inner sexual feelings about same sex preference. Now, just barely out of high school and becoming a young adult her struggling with her the feelings was becoming hard and harder to hide from mom and Dad. All of us siblings knew about it, but it was something no one talked about in front of our parents. Although, they did wonder now and then, why she never had any boy friends, she was a pretty girl.

Back in the mid 80s, the issue of same sex relationships no one talked about at least not publicly. Feelings bottled up for many years only to remain in the "closet," so to speak. She really had no guidance on how to handle the different emotions she was trying to fight. All she knew was she couldn't confide in our parents. Just the thought of facing them with her issue was more than she could bear. Her way of keeping it hidden was moving out of the house.

Normally moving out to live on your own is welcome among parents, but Dad knew she did not have a job and no place to live. He was aware she was heading down the wrong path with some friends she was hanging around and that wasn't helping her situation.

Dad was very headstrong when it came to issues like that. If he did not approve of the friends you were hanging around with, then they were gone and out of your life or else. Just the word or **else** was enough to keep most of us in line.

Although, that's where Dad and Sue started to butt heads. Sue did not want to hear that. Since she was not acting her normal self, those words only made her defensive, which made everything worse.

I will never forget that day; it was obvious to me she was not her sweet self. There was something seriously wrong with her disposition.

For Sue to stand up to Dad the way she did arguing as her temper only became worse was totally out of character for her. In her eyes, she was old enough to do what she wanted and no one was getting in her way. Because of Sue's low self-esteem, she became variable to her so-called friends. It was easy for them to influencing her with drinking and much more. I know she felt comfortable being around them; because it was her first real relationship with the same sexual preference. In her eyes she finally found someone that believe they way she did. Unfortunately, she started depending on them to guide her, sadly in the wrong direction.

To be honest with you the only issue Dad had with Sue hanging around with what he called the wrong crowd was the drinking problems. He never knew about Sue's other issues, it was never obvious to him. He would have put a stop to anyone that was leading any of his kids down the wrong path. Unfortunately, Sue took it the wrong way thinking Dad knew about her feelings, and she blew it all out of proportion.

The day she decided to approach mom and Dad to tell them she was moving out all hell broke out. Dad knew those so-called friends of hers were involved with her decision and he was very angry. Mom said she never saw Dad that mad at one of kids before.

When Dad started to ask her all kinds of questions about these "friends," it only made Sue defensive again. All her emotions Sue had stored up inside her came pouring out. He started putting on the pressure not understanding why she needed to hang around with those friends in the first place. Furthermore, he didn't understand why she needed to move out when she had a roof over her head now. He kept trying to convince her to wait until she had a good job so she could take care of herself.

It was then Sue said "that doesn't matter my girlfriend said she would take care of me." That's was all Dad needed to hear he blew up. He said "are you kidding me what do you mean your girlfriend!" At that moment Dad finally realized what Sue meant by "girlfriend." He was left off guard and didn't know how to handle that comment.

Mom and Dad had old-fashioned values, which certainly did not help the matter. In all fairness to them, it was not just their feelings. That certain type of life style in the mid 80s was a long way from being accepted. As mom left the room, Dad and Sue's voices got louder and louder. It became so loud mom quickly got on the phone and called me, only living 10 minutes away she knew I could get there before things got out of control.

When Sue was younger, she and I were very close even with the large 12 years difference in our ages. I was like her second mom. She always had a lot of respect for me and most of the time would listen to my advice.

When I pulled into their driveway, I could not believe the yelling that was coming from inside the house. Just as I walked in the door, I saw Sue and Dad face to face yelling at each other. She never did this before something was definitely strange with her. I yelled, "Sue stop," she looked at me and then ran out the door. The house became quiet as Dad just sat there with this terrible concerned look on his face thinking about what just happened. It definitely was out of character for him to get that upset especially at a daughter. Unfortunately, when Sue left home she never came back to the house to live.

Sue's troubles did get out of control. Still hanging around with the wrong crowd but now, she was on her own. Dad tried everything to get her on the right track. Even getting her a job at Ford Motor Company in hopes, she would calm down. Thank goodness, it worked; she and Dad mended their differences and she was on the verge of getting her life back on track shortly before he became ill.

Although it was hard for her to live day by day as she tried to stay sober, she was still very variable. It would only take one setback to start her addiction on all over again. Needless to say, Dad's illness was the "straw that broke her back". My sweet sister had this huge setback. She retreated to the only thing that could help her forget his disease—drinking and much more.

I know it was hard for her to face his illness especially realizing how much Dad did to help her get her life back on track. In her mind, if she did not come around the house very much to visit Dad, then she did not have to deal with his illness.

As I have said before, we were so engrossed in caring for him; we never noticed how bad mom or Sue's problems were. Our only concerns were about Dad he could not care for himself and they still could.

In the end, Dad would have been very proud of Sue. With the love of God and supporting friends and family, she became our **Sue again!**

You know, with all of these troubles going on in our family I couldn't help remembering what someone once told me in a comforting way. "God only gives you enough depressing situations in your life that he knows you're capable of handling." My only thought was he must have figured we were a very strong and capable family who could handle a lot because we certainly had **more** than our share.

For the most part our life was great, believe me I counted my blessings everyday. Even though from time to time I used to think to myself, life is not always perfect. Episodes do happen that cause many bumps in the road along your journey, which we have to accept. However, I did have a hard time dealing with "why it had to be dumped on us all at once!" I guess it's not up to us to question why!

CHAPTER 32

Our last chance for communication slowly dies

Still not being able to communicate with Dad was causing all types of problems. Yes, I know we were fortunate in the past with our communication hurdles every time managing to climb over them. Now, do I dare admit it was gone forever?

As I stood there looking at Dad lying in bed not being able to communicate any more for that was all he had left in his life to look forward to. It became impossible for me to see him go through these difficulties.

For when I looked straight into Dad's eyes trying hard to guess what he needed I felt the pressure of him trying to tell me something as if his eyes were piercing a whole right through me. Every time you could feel his wants however, you never knew what they meant. This became so frustrating for me. The more I would try to guess, straining my eyes trying to see some signs of a reply, the more I became depressed. As long as his equipment was working properly, there was not a damn thing I could do. Eventually I had to give up leaving the room in tears feeling as if I was letting my Dad down.

Deep down inside I knew he did not think that nevertheless, it was still hard for me to come to terms with it. Dad knew his family was not going to give up on him it was not in our nature. Even though we all knew his journey on his road of life was ending we still had to keep trying.

He was now at a very dangerous stage with his illness. At any point, unknown complications could compromise his immune system and cause his life. There was no doubt his health and his life was jeopardized without some type of communication.

Thank God for Denise his nurse. Since she had spent so much time with Dad throughout his illness, she had a handle on most of his needs and was able to relate them to the other nurses when they took over.

However, Dad was now having new health issues. His disease was rapidly progressing to the point that even his doctor was concerned. His house calls were more frequent and examinations more thorough. We certainly did not need any new health complications, since now we were back to the guessing game with his needs.

I will never forget this one day when the doctor was examining Dad. As he finished he decided to focus more on Dad's eyes explaining to us that if Dad's eyes were dilated he could tell if his body was in a stress situation, which was something he wanted us to watch for now. As he pulled out this high intense magnifying glass with a light to help him see clearly into his eyes he became puzzled. For a spilt second he thought Dad's one eye responded slightly to the light, which seemed very strange to him because it was the same eye, which Dad could blink before.

With excitement in his voice, he said, "I can't believe I'm seeing this I think your Dad's eye just moved." Just to make sure he looked again. He was right Dad's eye was actually following the light that was shining in at him although the movement was very weak. With that concern, we felt he was probably able to move it all this time and we never notice it, now maybe that movement was weaker also and we were too late. I have to say; in our defense, we were so excited to see him control his blinking before of course we didn't notice the movement in his eye. We were satisfied just to have any type of muscle movement and didn't have the need to look any further.

It's no wonder I felt Dad staring a hole right through me when I was asking him questions. It made me sick when I realized that he was hoping I would notice the movement in his eye before it was too late to take advantage of it. I was so upset with myself I should have been more aware of that, now it might be too late. The eye muscle was already weak. Still we wondered if there could be another way to use this new eye movement for communication. Only one person we knew who was able to help us, Daniel our engineering communication expert. It has been awhile since we last talked with him, hoping he had some new technology they could use for Dad.

We were excited to hear his medical company now had a new eye sensor switch that could activate a computer more efficiently, without interfering with anyone's vision. We knew that was only a matter of time until they perfected that.

Daniel wanted to come out to the house to see what was going on with Dad anyway. If indeed, he found Dad could move his eye enough to operate the new device maybe he said, it might just work.

Here we go again finding hope. It was then I truly believed God was with us throughout Dad's illness guiding us in these directions. He knew Dad was not going to get better so he gave us other roads to take to make his illness a little easier for us to handle.

The most important thing I have learned throughout this journey with our Dad was knowing we can feel proud that all our searching for help for him, in the end did paid off. Even though he was never going to get better, our team of professional experts we acquired along the way was **priceless.**

When Daniel examined Dad's eye, he was surprised with this new movement while cautioning the family at the same time not to get too excited. He made sure it was Dad controlling the movement and not twitching from the disease, which by now even that was going.

We had to look very hard to detect any movement at all. As we stood there waiting for Dad to respond, you could see his eye move slightly. For the family's sake, I think he was not only letting us know he could move it but also reassuring us that his mind was still alert and his vision and hearing weren't affected,—yet. This was something we feared was already happening. Again, our excitement was high only this time holding our breath, we knew the movement was very slight.

When we had the sensor switch in place, we all eagerly watched the screen for a response from Dad. At first, there was nothing. Then we remembered that we had the same problem last time until Dad got the knack of it so we patiently waited.

Daniel saw the worried look on our faces and said, "now lets don't jump the gun yet, let me adjust the switch a little closer to his eye." All of a sudden, we heard the sound of the computer activating the letters on the screen again, as Dad typed, **"I'm back."**

I know it must be hard to imagine all the chances we had for communication with Dad. However, whenever it seemed like one door would close, miraculously another one would open for us. Yet it did feel like we were stretching our luck and eventually it was going to run out. Because of that, we felt it was important for Dad to communicate to us about any new health complications we had no idea was going on with him. Especially wondering did he change his mind about taken him off the ventilator now. Since he had a taste of lack of communication, didn't that scare him?

Yes, Dad frantically did a lot of typing of things he wanted us to know with his affairs, as if he knew himself he was running out of time, but never did he type any demands about himself with the ventilator. I still could not understand that. You would have thought that would have been his number one priority.

Tension in the house was starting to build again. No matter how good we kept up his care, his illness was out of our control. For us not to be able to do anything about it was more than we could bear.

His digestive system was starting to breakdown, which was a sign the end was near. The feeding tube the doctor had inserted into his stomach when he was first immobile was starting to back up causing a lot of stress on his kidneys. His body was fighting hard just to stay alive. Even his bladder was backing up and when it's not emptying properly, its sets the stage for bacteria to set in. His doctor fully expected these problems would eventually happen, as he referred to them as a "ripple effect". Explaining to us, every organ relates to each other in some way. He was preparing us for what lay ahead of us.

I have to say for us to prepare ourselves was totally thinking out of the box, we never allowed our thoughts to go there before. We were always thinking of ways to help him and because of that, his life never was in distress.

Yet with all of these new health conditions happening to him, we still were in denial the end was near, and still **fought** for his life. Because of the way, we were feeling Dad's doctor knew it was going to be impossible for the family to brace ourselves for Dad's outcome. He did his best to make Dad as comfortable as possible for all our sakes.

Now Dad had no choice with having a catheter. To prevent damage to his kidney he had to have it. Having his bladder empty automatically now was important, that muscle was even gone. All that resolved was another tube sticking out of him.

If that wasn't enough agony, sadly when we looked into Dad's eyes all we could see there was a cloudy membrane starting to form, was his eye movement going now too? Still fooling ourselves maybe there was something that could correct it so he could continue with his communication. Even thinking at one point maybe it was cataracts causing the problem. That we knew could be corrected. Of course, never did we want to admit the disease was causing this destruction, which only meant one thing, **giving up!**

Just to reassure us it was not his disease causing his eye to cloud over we contacted an eye doctor to see if he could help. When we explained to the doctor about Dad's illness, he was more than willing to come to the house to do the exam. In the end to our despair, the doctor verified Dad's eye was deteriorating from the disease.

For us reality was now setting in. It was as if we were hit in the head with this huge rock and nothing could stop the bleeding. Was Dad's fight for communication finally over?

Throughout all of this, the unknown was the hardest for us to face. We never knew how to prepare for that. Always wondering if Dad would lose his vision just because he was losing his eye muscle movement, or even maybe his hearing was going also. We had no way to tell anymore. I finally had to admit to myself my positive attitude was fading away. **I was hitting rock bottom!** How do you try to remain focused on the good things?

Our family always bounced back before, even though this was going to be more of a challenge could we even think about stopping now? The only thing we knew we could do well was be more aggressive in pursuing other avenues of communication, we just couldn't stop, we didn't know how! We went back to Daniel and pleading for more help it was our only defense left.

After we contacted him again, and told him that Dad could not use his eye anymore, I remember him saying, "let's just wait, I think I may have one more approach we might be able to pursue for your Dad." He always made us feel good always encouraging us not to give up yet. It was a blessing to have this man in our life.

By now, he was very familiar with Dad's health. He certainly knew how his body responded. Since he had all the knowledge about muscle skills and how to take advantage of their movement, he was aware of one more area on his body that may still have an active muscle called a sphincter. As I let out this big sigh and told him anatomy was never my best subject in school, could you please explain "what in the world was a sphincter muscle?"

I was amazed as he describe it as he explained, "it's a ring shaped muscle at the end of the orifice, which is the opening around the anus that enables the movement of your bowels." You know when you think about the human body and what it's capable of doing certainly is remarkable, something you never give a second thought to until you're in a situation like Dads. He went on to say "if your Dad is still capable of controlling his bowel movements, which we don't know for sure, meant only one thing an active muscle, which of course means a new source of movement to focus on."

He tried to explain a little future saying, "with this disease to have any control of any muscle was a plus even if it meant that area. This new device inserted into a patient anus is to detect movement. If it's successful even that movement will control the computer. He said they already used it on a patient with the similar condition as Dads.

It did not take him long to get back with that information for us. Unfortunately, there was one drawback with this procedure knowing the family may have a problem with it. If this is going to work, it's important to see if your Dad's sphincter muscle is functioning properly. We need to perform the test in a sterile environment so he either has to be in our lab, or a hospital. We need to do an EMG, electromyogram test on his nerve to see if there is activity.

What a major decision this was for the family. Daniel knew how hard we had worked to keep Dad out of environments like that because of issues with germs.

As we thought about it realizing this may be Dad's last chance for communication ever again. Trying to weigh the difference whether we wanted to take the risk after everything we had been through already trying to keep Dad healthy. Was this worth the risk now? **Even if it meant it was his last chance!**

This is when we thought mom should have the final say. For us to interfere this time was wrong. Letting her know she had our full support was the right thing to do. However, it backfired on us. This "straw broke her back."

Instead of being a leader, she started to shut down. It was more than she could bear. Enough was enough. She was done and ready to give up. It got to the point she did not trust herself to make any decision for Dad's health anymore. Her mind was starting to get frazzled and confused. Just the thought of making a wrong decision was going to send her over the edge. If that happened then we would have two parents to take care of.

The reality was I could not blame her for feeling that way. Mom never had to make any serious decision before. Dad was always there to take charge. He was the main decision maker in the family, so in her defense never was she put in that position. Now with the physical crutch she had with her drinking, only made things worse.

Dad was aware this could happen someday to mom especially knowing if something happened to him she would need a lot of mental support. Giving joint power of attorney to Jim and mom together was the decision he made way before he became ill. Hoping she would have Jim to lean would help to build up her confidence—**so we thought!**

As we watched mom meltdown with this decision, we realized she couldn't do it alone. We had to step in and help her with it. Being a **FAMILY** this responsibility was all of ours. Never did we want any one person to feel guilty if it came down to the wrong decision. All along hoping, we were making the right choice.

In the end, we were wrong; taking the pressure off mom did not help her with her wellbeing. In fact, she was already at her wits end all this did was add to it. I think she was hoping we would have just left well enough alone, although she never told us that but it was obvious.

The reality was she knew the end was near for Dad, she was done with chasing rainbows a long time ago, and she was just waiting for us to realize it. Having to make this decision only gave her more reason to drink, which by now was all the time. How were we supposed to know that would happen? We thought we were doing the right thing. After all, we did overstep our boundaries with the nursing home decision; we did not want to make the same mistake again.

That did not help mom her spirit was now broken. She got to the point her days did not mean anything to her anymore. It seemed like all she wanted to do was retreat to her bedroom and stay there all day long, justifying the reason she did not have to face any responsibilities.

She was trying hard to find sanctuary in her room as she tried to block out all the noise in the living room from the machines that were keeping Dad alive. Giving us the excuse all she wanted was to enjoy her books or watch her TV shows. She did not even want to talk to us. All she wanted to do was curl up inside herself, as her bedroom slowly became her retreat.

What worried us the most was it did not take very long when she was in her room for her to be sound asleep in bed, always with the blankets pulled up over her head as if it helped to block out the whole world, especially the sounds of Dad's life support.

The changes in her were becoming more apparent everyday. Even the grandkids started noticing her personality changing especially the older ones, which was hard for them to deal with.

Unfortunately, for them it did get to the point it became harder for them to go over to mom and Dad's house anymore. Even though they both were still with us, it was not their grandparents any more. They felt they were losing both of them.

That was sad for me to see. I felt the only way for my two daughters to deal with this was to make them visit. Thinking as a parent, I was making the right decision. Many years later my oldest daughter Kimberly, told me how much it hurt her to see her grandparents in that condition.

Kimberly and Kristie always valued family traditions highly; it was the way they were raised. However, Kimberly was the one who always had the hardest time with changes. Admitting her life at grandma and grandpa's was not the same anymore. She told me she did regret that she we forced her to see them; later on in her life, she had nightmares about it. Only at the time, I thought she would have regretted for the rest of her life if she did not see them. **Being a parent, you always hope you make the right decisions when it comes to your children sometimes the best intentions get misguided.**

Now when the older grandkids got together as they reminisce about all the good times they had growing up and going to grandma and grandpa's house were fond memories for them, which left a huge impression in their hearts.

Unfortunately, younger grandkids never had the chance to know them in that way. Nevertheless, they enjoyed listening to all the stories told by the older ones.

I have to say as the debate continued with this decision for Dad's last chance for communicate, as I watched him fighting to stay alive to just lay there with no hope only made me more determined to make my mind up to go for it. To be able to communicate again was all he had left in his life.

Over and over, we tried to persuade mom not to give up on Dad trying to convince her we still had hope left. We needed to see if this last means of communication could work for him. I know her mind was going was in a different direction and she did not care about the communication any more, after all it had been almost three years since he was on ventilator care. I 'm sure she was thinking if we did find another way to communicate with Dad it would not last long, so why be so aggressive anymore? She knew he was reaching the end of his life.

The sad thing about all of this was she was right. It was us kids, we were not ready to let him go. We were still living in a dream. We could never fathom the thought of giving up on him. Because of the sad looks on our faces mom gave in again. I now wonder if we did the right thing trying to be persistent. One thing I have learned throughout all of this you cannot turn back the clock when you have regrets.

The next day after all that disputing, we agreed to go ahead with his last chance for communication. We wanted Dad to have the EMG test only if it was in the outpatient lab not the hospital. Thinking maybe the lab was the lesser of the two places exposing him to germs. Mom went along with the decision, but I know her mind was going in a different direction.

CHAPTER 33

The last straw for Mom,
only enhances her giving up

Our final hope was October 1987 when we contacted Daniel again, we told him of our decision, he agreed with us having the procedure done in the lab was probable the wisest decision. Daniel contacted his friend and co-worker who developed this switch Dr. Smith her expertise was important for Dad. We also contacted Dad's neurologist since we always kept him abreast of everything. Of course, we hoped he would be there also just in case Dad had physical issues while he was having this test, which would put us all at ease.

The procedure did not take long, however for us sitting in the waiting room for some news about him felt like forever. No one wanted to think the worse although silently it was on all of our minds.

As I glanced towards mom, you could see she was exhausted. She nodded her head a couple of times as if she was falling asleep. She looked so worn and frail; her tiny body was just as thin as she could be. Her cough was getting worse.

Watching her whole body shake as she coughed made me mad enough to make a negative comment about her smoking again. I really felt bad after I said it but everyone's tensions were so high, all I could think of was having two parents dying.

I found myself raising my voice when I told her, "mom look at yourself, your immune system is stressed out with all your smoking," as if I was scolding her. I know that was the wrong place to speak about her smoking, but frankly, I was mad she was causing her own illness. Here we spent so much time looking for something to help Dad all she had to do was stop smoking. I guess I was just a little upset.

I will never forget her reply to me. She looked right at me and kind of laughed and said, "do you really think it's the smoking that's stressing my body?"

At that point, I figured she was right and whatever happened to her now just did not matter to her anymore. She was losing her best friend, her lover, her companion of 40 years and she did not care about herself. It was then I realized she was preparing for the worse. I think she was the only one who was.

I remember in the very beginning of Dad's illness mom was the only one who knew there was no hope with this disease. Having been there before with grandma, still she never could convince us of that.

Sitting in the waiting room going over everything we had gone through in the last three years, I started fuming thinking how mom seemed to have fought us all the way with Dad's care. My mind was racing with all kinds of negative thoughts. Thinking how much mom had pushed for the nursing home situation from the very start. After all, I thought to myself we did have 24 hour nursing care covered. What more could she want? To me that was being selfish on her part. I felt a nursing home situation was just an easy way out of taken care of a loved one yourself. Then I thought, that's a harsh statement to make since I can't be the judge of that, I wasn't speaking from experience. You never know until you have walked in their shoes.

I had to get those thoughts out of my mind. Never did I want to have negative thoughts towards my mom. Was I breaking down too and blaming everything on her? Shame on me, I was tired and drained also. Thank God, they were just thoughts. I could not bear to hurt her feelings. She was hurting enough.

Many years later as I look back, I realize we were the selfish ones. We had normal lives to go home to sadly mom had no place to go but to her retreat, her bedroom. At the time, we had blindfolds on. Again, thinking with your heart does not lead you in the right direction.

Still waiting for the doctor to come out of the examining room and give us some news about Dad's procedure the door slowly opened. The look on the doctor's face told us everything.

When he told us the results of Dad's test, all he could do was apologize repeatedly as if he took it hard also. I remember those haunting words as he said, "I'm so sorry to tell you this but when we checked out your Dad's sphincter muscle it didn't show any signs of cortical activity." This meant the disease had taken over that muscle too.

I just sat there in a daze thinking now what! For the first time in Dad's illness, we had no more choices there was nothing left to do. All I wanted to do was take Dad home right away. I felt as long as he was at home the thought of him being there would comfort me. Again, I was only thinking about myself. I couldn't handle the thought of Dad being gone. You could sense the depression was hitting him too.

Mom felt helpless for her children and there wasn't anything she could do. She knew in the end we would eventually come crashing down and she could not provide a safety net to catch us. Now we were finally admitting Dad's demise.

With all of this going on with Dad, I had the weirdest feeling about mom's coughing. I know there was something going on with her that day she was never one to snap at any of us. However, I could not put my finger on it. Was she on the verge of telling me something when I was nagging her about her smoking that day in the waiting room? Then changing her mind as she realized it was not the time to say anything to us after seeing our hopes for Dad vanish.

Here she was just like a mom trying to protect her kids. She knew how much pain we were all going through now with facing Dad's demise. She did not want to add to our burden. I truly think this last episode with Dad since all hope for him was gone, only gave her something constructive to concentrate on again, us her children, which made her feel needed again.

When we got Dad home and settled in my thoughts started wandering. I now had to come to terms with the fact that soon Dad wouldn't be in our lives anymore. As I stood in their living room with all of those thoughts racing in my mind, I could not imagine the kind of thoughts that were going through his. Truly now there was no doubt he was facing death.

I could not help wondering if he was sorry, he never communicated to us about his wishes about the ventilator. How could he just lay there with no hope anymore? It was making me sick inside thinking about it. Nevertheless, what could we do?

CHAPTER 34
A desperate family facing two parent's demise

Now with no more hope for him and seeing how poorly mom's health was becoming. Feeling guilty maybe, he was the one that was causing it. I do believe this is when Dad started to give into this disease.

Yes, mom's cold was getting worse nevertheless, she did get this cold every year around the same period so in our defense we figured it was the smoking causing it to get worse. Although this time, her coughing was not getting better. Lucky for us we had Denise around keeping an eye on Dad and now mom. That's all the family needed two parents sick.

Just to make sure mom's cold was not turning into something else; we made an appointment for her to see her doctor. Hoping at the same time, he could address the issue of her drinking problem. Thank goodness, she did not know what we were planning. I'm sure if she knew she would have refused to go see him.

Her doctor knew the family well, and was aware of everything that was going on at home. In fact, he was the one who would come out to the house to check on Dad before we had his neurologist.

The relationship mom had with her doctor was special. In a sense, he became her therapist at the same time. When mom would go in for her normal check- up, she was always his last patient of the day. He knew how hectic it was at home for her so after her appointment he just sat and listened to her. It was great therapy for mom.

Throughout their talks, he was always aware of her drinking however, I am sure she never told him how much. Maybe this is why he never had any reason to panic until we finally told him it was getting out of control.

With mom, not hesitating to see him was a plus for us. It was the perfect opportunity for him to convince her to stop drinking. Not knowing what their talk was going to be about she wouldn't have her guard up when she saw him.

When I took mom to her appointment, it felt like she was in his office for a long time. When the door opened, I thought she was done however; it was the doctor wanting to show me an x-ray of mom's lungs.

They were cloudy and he was concerned of pneumonia. He told me she needed to go in the hospital for more tests. Mom did not argue with him, I think she was glad she was going to be gone from the house for a couple of days. In fact, she was looking forward to having her meals in bed, even if it meant staying in the hospital.

I think she was the only person in the world who never complained about hospital food. Maybe that was how desperate she was to have a break from all the chaos going on at home. It worked out good for us with Dad. Denise decided to stay over night for the week until mom was home and back on her feet.

After her tests were back and the pneumonia cleared up, mom looked rejuvenated. The stay in the hospital did her some good. She was ready to come home and face the end to Dad's life without any remorse, realizing our only alternative was making him as comfortable as possible.

When mom's doctor called me and said, we needed to have a family meeting to discuss her health I was excited. Finally, in my mind I thought he wanted to talk about her drinking. I certainly was wrong!

I guess in his defense I never gave him a chance to explain what he meant by her health. All along, I was assuming the talk was going to be about her drinking, since the pneumonia had cleared up. Never did we have a chance to prepare for what he had to tell us. It was imperative to him that everyone in the family be there.

When I called everyone and told them of the doctors meeting most of my siblings were as excited as I was. Still we thought he was going to address the issue of mom's drinking.

With Sue knowing what our plan was going to be she felt guilty about coming since she too was still fighting her own demons. After a long time of trying to convince her, she finally promised to be there.

It is hard to find the right words to tell you what happened at the meeting. When I think about that day, it still leaves me in shock.

Here we all were sitting in the doctor's office in a circle of chairs. Sue was sitting way over in a corner by herself. I tried telling her to come and sit by me so I could put my arms around her to give her some comforting support however, all she did was push me away. To this day, I regretted not being next to her when the doctor came out of his office for his talk.

As soon as the doctor came in the room, he was carrying mom's x-rays in his hands. I thought to myself why does he need those to talk about her drinking. Right then my heart sank as I held my breath waiting to hear what he had to say next. The room became very quiet as he stood there trying to find the right words before he spoke. Then he said as he held up this folder "these are the results of your mother's tests she had while in the hospital."

It was then I knew this was not going to turn out very well. All I could think of is why did I put the family in this position? I should have asked more questions before we had this meeting. As I remember what happened to me when I was with Dad with his first diagnosis praying this wasn't going to turn out the same way. I started feeling numb all over not knowing what to expect. I was afraid to look around the room and make eye contact with any of my brothers and sisters for fear they would see the puzzled look on my face.

When the doctor continued he held up the x-ray, again my heart sunk. I knew this was not going to be a good scene. He said, "I have a disturbing picture of your mom's lung." Then, out came the big *"C"*

215

word, "your mom has a very large tumor in her lungs, unfortunately it's malignant. This type of cancer is fast spreading. I'm sorry to tell you this, unfortunately your mother has only six months to live." That is when all hell broke out and started a panic among us!

When I looked over towards Sue to try to console her she jumped out of her chair and ran out of the office. I tried to catch her but she had a friend waiting for her out in the parking lot. She jumped into the car and off they went burning rubber as they rushed out of the parking lot. I stood there crying wondering if she was going to be alright.

What a shock it was for all of us. All along, we were preparing ourselves for this intervention to happen over mom's drinking, only to have this bomb dropped in our laps. I was feeling guilty for not preparing my brothers and sisters ahead of time although, this news left me off guard too.

I know all of this was not the doctor's fault as he stood there looking very somber with all this chaos going on in his office. I blame this on myself. All along, I was thinking he was going to talk to us about her drinking. I never knew mom was that sick. At least I could have had a chance to prepare the family. I felt like I let them down that day.

As if Dad's illness was not enough now we had mom's health to think of too. How much can one family deal with, now we were facing another parent dying. It was becoming hard to remain focus anymore.

The doctor told us mom already knew the bad news while she was in the hospital. She never said anything to us thinking it would be easier coming from the doctor. I cannot imagine her hearing that diagnosis all by herself with no support from anyone. I know it was her decision to make however; I still was upset she was alone when she heard it. How could she have kept something as serious as that to herself?

After hearing the terrible news from the doctor, all we could think of was getting back to their house to be with mom. She needed our love and support right now.

When we pulled in the driveway, we could see into the kitchen. There she sat all alone with tears running down her face waiting to see how we were going to react when we heard the bad news. As she feared how she was going to handle our depression when we came in the door.

As she watched us walk in the door with our heads hanging down her tears worsen. She was not crying for herself they were tears for her children. Never was she concerned about her illness her concerns were for her children. Can you imagine her feeling like that just like a mother?

As we ran in to give her a hug, crying at the same time she tried to hush our voices so Dad would not hear what was going on. All of a sudden, her tears stopped and we saw this inner strength come pouring out of her as if she was rejuvenated having this inner body experience giving her strength to carry on.

Here mom was on the verge of a mental breakdown with everything that was happening to Dad. Now she was facing her own demise and she was stronger than ever.

I was amazed and had a hard time understanding what just happened to her. She was a completely different person. I think her strength was coming from up above, it was the only way I could make any sense out of it. She was more concerned about Dad knowing about her illness than how she felt about it herself. She told us she needed some time to find the right words to tell Dad as she tried to protect him.

I could not believe this was my mom. What an amazing women she became that day. Even with her crutch, her addiction, for the first time since Dad's illness we actually saw her inner strength.

In a weird sense, I actually think she was content she was going to die. She knew her motherly job was through with us kids and she did not want to be all alone without Dad. Throughout Dad's illness, I think it weighed heavily on her mind. She did not know how she was going to go on without him. Now she did not have to find out. You could tell she was at peace knowing that.

I was very proud of mom's strength that day and sad at the same time because now we were losing her too. Now our mom was dealing with her own death and did not have her husband to lean on for support. As a family, we needed to regroup to figure out what to do for her.

Wanting mom to start cancer treatment was out of the question for her. "Why do I want to prolong the inevitable she said?" She watched our family go through Dad's illness and knew she was not doing that to us again. However, in our eyes how could we not help one parent and ignore the other it was not fair. After all our pleading, she finally gave in.

I remember taking her to the hospital for radiation treatment. She said as long as it did not make her sick she would go through it. There I was again with another parent sitting in the hospital waiting room. My only remembrance of being there was this vision of her walking around the waiting room in her frail little body making friends with all the other patients who were waiting for their own treatment. She found herself comparing types of cancer with them and was consoling everyone else at the same time. I was truly overwhelmed with her unselfish compassion.

With mom given six months to live, Jim realized he had his hands full. He knew he had to get this family organized fast.

Knowing he was responsible to help mom, and knowing Dad wanted him to take charge of the family affairs if mom couldn't, was playing heavily on his mind now. I'm sure he felt he never would have be in this position, however here he was. Moreover, if that wasn't enough pressure, he realize there was a very tough road ahead especially with our big family.

Now there were decisions that had to be made that were going to be nearly impossible, although, he knew he had no choice. In the back of Jim's mind, he knew we could not take Dad off the ventilator legally now. There wasn't any documentation stating his wish on that issue. Jim knew the family only had one option with the rest of his care. Unfortunately, it was a nursing home. There's no way our family could struggle taking care of two parents it would have torn us apart.

Jim has always been a sensible man. Always thinking with his mind and trying to leave his heart out of the decision. At times, I was upset with him for that because he was so level headed. Nevertheless, in the end I was grateful he was so strong. Dad knew Jim would know what to do; he was so much like Dad.

The hardest part of Jim's job was trying to convince the family the need of the nursing home for Dad. In the past, we were closed mined about the idea. Just like anything else when there were disagreements among us we had family meetings. The most important issue now for Jim was keeping the mentality of the family together. Everyone had their own views on how things should be handled. That's the only drawback with a large family. Thank God, Jim was highly respected among the brothers and sisters. Along with my help, we kept the sanity in the family, and faced the hardest decision we ever had to make—**nursing home!** It was our only option. Mom was in total agreement with the decision from the start and was very relieved it was finally made.

In the meantime, after a couple treatments of radiation mom decided it was making her to sick. There was no way she wanted that to happen. She wanted her mind to be alert so she could be in charge with everything that was going on for as long as she could. Keeping up her strength was very important to her. There was too much for her to do now especially with organizing the family affairs. I have to say, this attitude totally surprised us all.

That is when Linda started to look into alternative treatments for her cancer, just as she did with Dad illness. She read many positive things about a cancer clinic in Mexico that was doing treatments for patients especially with lung cancer, which was not approved yet in the U.S., yet. Linda felt it was a great place for mom to go.

I was in the room when she told mom about it. When I heard mom's response, "**WHAT, ARE YOU CRAZY,**" I just chuckled to myself knowing she was going to say that. Mom thought for a second then changed her mind saying, "well okay maybe I can treat this as one last vacation for me." That really made me laugh, for I knew that was my mom." Linda did not tell her until they got there that this was not going to be a fancy hotel. I am glad I was not there when she found out!

Mom knew at this point there was nothing else she could do for Dad, she was at peace with herself knowing he was getting quality care at home. Whatever happened to him while she was gone was out of her control.

Although, before she left, she wanted to tell Dad about her cancer and that she was going to this clinic for treatments. Never did she tell him how serious it was until the day Dad was on his deathbed.

At this stage in Dad's illness, we did not know if he could still see or hear us. Nevertheless, mom knew he would sense her being gone. When she whispered in his ear telling him about her illness, it was a very touching scene. Knowing she did not have long on this earth either she was okay with it, because Dad would not be alone for long.

It was November 1987, mom wanted to get this Mexico trip done so she could get Dad settled in a nursing home before Christmas. She knew his time was near; and she never wanted him to die at home.

When I was a little child, she remembered me having terrible nightmares over my grandma dying in our home. She did not want her grandkids having those same thoughts. Even though it was not their home, it would still leave haunting images in their minds.

When she left for Mexico, Bob, Rick and Linda went with her. In the meantime, Jim and I went on this terrible search looking for nursing homes for Dad. I would have rather gone to Mexico even though I hated flying.

Mom certainly got a wake up call when she got to the clinic. In the first place, it was in the middle of nowhere and it definitely had no room service. It certainly was not what she expected.

She even had to give up her beer because the first thing they did to her was detoxify her body. Linda said the place was amazing. Everything they put mom through kept her pain free. She did not know what they used but it worked. I used to tease mom saying I am sure it was some illegal drugs. Now 22 years later it's becoming the sought out cure all, with the debate still questioning its legalities. Nevertheless, mom's response to my comment was "**PAMELA.**" I always knew I was in trouble when she called me "Pamela" and not Pam.

Linda made sure the family back home knew mom was safe and in the right place. It was funny with my two brothers going along. I'm not sure they were much help for Linda since she was doing all the work. Maybe they were just their bodyguards. On the other hand, if the truth were known maybe it was the free ride. Whatever it was it reassuring for Linda and mom they were there and that's what counted.

Although, I have to laugh, when my brothers ran into this old time western movie star who was also receiving treatment there, you should have heard the excitement in their voice. Now here were two grown men very excited over an old and used to be famous western movie star.

Back when we were kids, my brothers use to drive me crazy with all the cowboy movies they watched. They knew this man name and the title of his TV western show and could not wait to get his autograph, which was all they talked about when they came home. **Who cared?** At least it broke up the tension. I was surprised they even recognized him; I think the man was in his eighties. That just proves how much cowboy shows they watched.

CHAPTER 35
The end of Dad's journey—Nursing Home

While mom was in Mexico, Jim and I started our search for a nursing home. With everything, we went through with Dad's illness this was my worst nightmare.

Here I was bragging about our never giving up family attitude, now I felt like a hypocrite facing a nursing home for Dad. It made me sick to my stomach. I would go home at night and not talk to anyone. I was mentally run down, and could not eat. Again, just like when I found out about Dad's illness, all I wanted to do was curl up inside myself and have everyone leave me alone. I could not come to terms with putting Dad in a nursing home, even though I knew it was the best situation for everyone.

Jim was becoming concerned for me and wanted to relieve my stress feeling it was better if he continued searching for a nursing home by himself. There was no way I was going to let him be stuck with that decision. Furthermore, I knew I had to face it eventually.

If you have ever been in that situation I am sure you can relate to what I was going through. The minute we stepped in the door of a nursing home and you smelled the odor of urine, I refused to go further. **I felt like throwing up!** To be honest with you what I really felt like doing was going home to drink my depression away. Of course, I never did that I knew better. Nevertheless, I was feeling guilty thinking I was deserting my Dad. To me all I was doing was letting him down. Over and over again, Jim tried to talk some sense into me. You see, I was thinking with my heart, how could I not, he was my Dad.

What made our search even more difficult there were not enough nursing homes capable of accepting ventilator patients at least not in 1987 in Michigan. Another problem we encountered that we did not agree with was their obligation to treat patients for every complication, which I understood, but not when they were on their deathbed, that seems inhumane. Of course, we wanted Dad pain free however; never could we live with ourselves knowing all we were doing was prolonging his life in a **nursing home.** I am sure things have changed hopefully, now that it's 2011.

In the end, we found a nursing home in Ohio, just past the Michigan and Ohio border. A friend of Jim's told him of this wonderful nursing home that was family owned. The feeling it gave us was a home away from home. The importance they put on the family feeling comfortable when you came to visit and the wonderful kind care they gave your loved ones was important to them as it was to us. After all that was the hardest part for a family to deal with. Talk about being clean, I could not believe it! Never did you smell the order of urine, **NEVER!** I know most of us felt at peace with Dad going there nevertheless; I was still fighting my guilt.

Another reason that convinced us to choose this nursing home was the way they honored our wishes about no resuscitating if he went into cardiac arrest. That in itself was very difficult for me to come to terms with, I knew we had to make that demand, but still it made me feel as if we were the ones who were responsible for his death.

When mom came home from Mexico, I could not help noticing how good she looked. Whatever treatments she had in the clinic really kept her pain in line. Not once was she all "dopey" from taking too much medication. If nothing else, at least it gave her a few more months of quality time to be with her family.

First thing, mom wanted to do was see the nursing home we chose for Dad. We all tried to convince her there was no rush after all she just got home. Nevertheless, we could not stop her determination. She had a strong feeling it needed to do it right away. Her concerns now were for her children, knowing everything should be in order for our sakes.

It was two weeks before Christmas, December 1987. A day I try not to remember, yet the haunting memories still linger, admitting Dad to the nursing home in Ohio. Everyone went along that day except me. Personally, I never wanted to see Dad in that place **ever,** even though in my heart, it was the right decision and his quality of care was excellent, I did not want my lasting memories of him to be in a nursing home. I knew it would haunt me for the rest of my life. My heart was in denial that Dad was approaching the end of his life. Although my mind knew better, nevertheless, I could not go.

That year I lost the memory of Christmas totally. It always was a very celebrated holiday in our family. Still to this day, I can't remember the Christmas of 1987. The harder I try to remember the more disturbed I become. Everything is just a blank. **I wonder why!**

The next couple of weekends the family continued to visit Dad, but I still refused to go with them. All I wanted was to be alone. Jim was worried that someday I would regret not going to say goodbye to my Dad so he tried his best to convince me every time they went. Still I refused. I could not bear to see my Dad in that place. I was being stubborn.

Christmas had passed and it was January 2nd 1988. I remember thinking some New Year! Everyone was getting ready to go and visit Dad. We all met at mom's house so we could drive down together. Still my family tried to convince me to go with them; I just sat in mom's living room dwelling in my grief looking at an empty hospital bed. Most of Dad's equipment went with him but the bed it was still there sitting **empty.**

When I looked around the room remembering all the complicated times we had struggling with communication for him, and how many hurdles we had to climb over to succeed only made me sadder. My Dad was still alive however; my heart was bleeding because I knew he soon would be gone. Now, I was losing my mom too. Thinking to myself, how in the world does a person get through all of this?

My life was changing rapidly. I knew I was going to face this huge gap, feeling sorry for myself. I even started thinking about where my two daughter's lives were going. In a sense, they were leaving me too, but in a good way. Still, it didn't stop the emptiness I was feeling.

Kristie was graduating from high school in the spring and soon would be going off to college. Kim was finishing her associate degree in nursing, also in the spring, and was leaving to live on her own. Jim had a new job keeping him very busy, which Dad always enjoyed hearing about it sadly; he was not there to tell him.

It was cold outside and snowing. I guess that is what you expect to happen in Michigan in January. Nevertheless, I was feeling depressed and all alone. Still, with all of that going through my head my family did not want to give up on me, trying very hard to convince me to go with them.

Just then, I saw this dove land on mom and Dad's deck, in the middle of winter no less. As I sat there watching it felt like he was looking right into their living room at me. It was a strangest feeling almost as if he was trying to tell me something. I knew right then it was a sign telling me to go and see Dad. I jumped up so fast and headed towards the car, never giving anyone a reason why I changed my mind, I just got in the car. I know Jim was puzzled but he never asked any questions he was just relieved I was going.

Even though in my heart I felt it was the right decision to make, the memory of my Dad dying in a nursing home is such a haunting lasting image, that it's hard to think of him in any other way, no matter how hard I try to block it out, it's as vivid as if it just happened.

The car ride on the way there was very quiet. Jim knew I was having strange feelings. In my heart, I just knew the end was now for Dad.

When we got to the nursing home, we pretty much had the whole family with us. The staff immediately stopped us from going into Dad's room telling us he was having serious complications that were affecting his life now. The doctor cautioned us on what we were going to see, telling us "your father's body is shutting down and it's only a matter of time until he passes on." Still hearing those words, I was not prepared to see him. The last time I saw Dad he was at home. He looked so youthful and handsome with a creamy complexion I was expecting no less.

When I walked into Dad's room and saw him lying there all bloated, I broke down crying uncontrollably. I notice Dad's eyes were closed, which we thought all his muscles were gone so how could that happen? His skin was all gray, and for a second I even doubted if I walked into the right room. Wondering what happened to him I excitedly said in a quivering voice, **that's not my Dad laying there it doesn't even look like him**. I had a hard time trying to stop from crying. I knew this was going to hit me hard; nevertheless, I couldn't prepare myself. After caring for Dad for the last three years reality was now setting in for me.

The doctor tried to explain what was happening to Dad as gently as he could, "when a loved one's time is near," he said, "especially in your Dad's case with his body being immobile for a long time, your bladder gets impacted causing swelling all over. His organs are no longer functioning as they too shutdown. His breathing is labored which in turn is causing his heart rate to slow down."

He said, "even at this point your Dad probably is not aware you're here." I was not ready to believe that. There is no doubt in my mind Dad knew we were with him that day. As I looked over to the side of his bed, there stood mom, not once did she breakdown she was so strong. As she bent down to give Dad a kiss, she whispered something in his ear. "Mom" I said, "What did you just say to Dad it looked like he had a tiny smile on his face." I know it was probably my imagination playing tricks on me, but she told me she saw it too.

When mom told me what she said I lost it. **"I told your father it was okay to go now. The doctor said my cancer is very serious and they only give me six months to live, soon I will be with you again."** I have no doubt after he heard that Dad was ready to let go.

That night no one wanted to go home so we all went to a hotel close by. I have always been a good sleeper however, that night I do not remember closing my eyes; I just kept watching the clock.

In the middle of the night, the phone rang. Jim got out of bed to answer it. All along, I was pretending I was sleeping so I did not have to get up and face reality. I heard Jim talking to the doctor and I knew my loving Dad was gone. I know Jim did not want to wake me thinking I was still sleeping; he just got into bed and held me tightly in his arms for the rest of the night.

I can remember my pillow being all wet from my tears but they were silent tears. I never wanted Jim to know I was awake and crying all night. I wasn't ready to face my Dad's death yet, even though I knew he was gone.

As I watched the sun rising as it peaked through the crack in the curtains, I knew that eventually I would have to get up and face the unbearable fact about Dad death. I was really hoping when I woke up I would have found all of this to have been a bad dream, a nightmare from the very beginning and everything was back to normal. Our family, our lives, our Sunday dinner traditions were back. **Life was good again.**

CHAPTER 36
Saying goodbye

Sadly, I was not dreaming at all. I had to get out of bed and face reality my biggest hurdle yet. One I knew would be impossible to get over, **saying goodbye to my Dad.**

Never in my worst nightmare did I prepare myself for this. Yes, Dad had the most horrific disease anyone could ever imagine and was ill for three long years. Therefore, you would have thought I was ready to let him go. In my eyes, I still felt a miracle would happen and there would be a cure. Maybe I was living in a dream world, although, at the time it was the only way I could mentally survive.

Yes, we were always searching for hope so reality of his disease never existed for me. I was not ready to give him up. All I knew for sure was my heart was bleeding and I could not imagine ever getting back to normal. I was in a daze with everything finding myself only going through the motions.

As depressed, as I was I told Jim we might as well reserve the funeral home right now for mom while planning for Dads. He knew how bad I was hurting so he ignored my comment.

When the word got out about Dads death, it seemed like the mail person was delivering sympathy cards for about a week while the phone was ringing off the hook.

Making funeral arrangements for Dad was a nightmare. Here I was falling apart and mom was holding me up. It was as if she was in someone else's body. I could not believe her strength. As mom planned for Dad's funeral, it was very important to her that his obituary be in all the major newspapers with a separate notice going to Ford Motor Company Body Engineering Division. She put the strongest emphasis on that.

Since mom had gone through so much with Dad's illness, we were all concerned for her emotional state of mind and did not want her run down any further, since she had a battle of her own to fight.

That did not faze mom at all; she was never concerned for her own health. I really did not think she cared she was dying. You know, I have always felt if mom were not dying from cancer she would have died from a broken heart with Dad no longer in her life. In my parent's generation, it seemed to me that the wife was very dependent on her husband. Even though my mom was out in the working world before she was married, when she settled down and had children the family became her life.

I was overwhelm with the way mom took charge of Dad's funeral, I couldn't have been any prouder. Mom certainly knew what she wanted and no one was going to hold her back.

I remember when she chose a hall for the luncheon after the service. Her main priority was it had to be large enough to accommodate many people. I never understood her decision on that one, since Dad had been sick for a while and away from the working environment.

I told mom there is no doubt he was very popular among his friends and co-workers when he was working, but it had been three years. People do have a tendency to forget when you are no longer around, out of sight out of mind.

Nevertheless, my theory wasn't going to change mom's mind, she kept on insisting over and over again that she needed to be prepared. "That's the way your Dad would have handled it."

I think in a way she was treating this like a retirement party Dad never had because of his illness. Mom wanted Dad to have this grand sendoff what could we say. It made her happy so we all agreed; after all, we were proud of what he had accomplished in his life also.

I will never forget the first day of the viewing. The funeral home seemed to have had a revolving door. The parking lot was stop and go traffic. They almost needed someone out there controlling the flow of traffic. I would have never believed it if I did not see it with my own eyes mom was right.

You should have seen how proud she was as she greeted everyone with this big smile on her face. Walking around in her frail little body with her head held up high, she never shed a tear or never sat down once. She had this gracious glow about her. So many kind and admiring words were spoken about Dad that day my throat was sore from talking so much.

I was in a daze of wonderment. Hearing about Dad and his work made me beam with pride, a side of him I never knew until he became ill.

Service was at 11:00 the following day and in the middle of the week no less. Mom did find a hall that could accommodate about 200 people. I was still insisting she did not need to accommodate so many. After all, I said, "we did see everyone yesterday. On top of that, we did live about 30 miles away from Dad's office, which is an awful long drive for someone's lunch hour even if they could take the time off from work.

All she said was "your father's final party will be grand just like he was." Every time we tried to convince her she was doing too much, we heard those words again. Who were we to argue with that? In the end mom was right. She knew exactly what she was doing. Here I though she was letting her heart and pride get in the way with common sense decisions.

As people came piling into the funeral home for the service it became obvious to the staff that they had to open up the adjourning rooms to accommodate everyone. Right before the service started Jim had to make a quick call to the hall to let them know they need to prepare for **300** people. I could not believe it there were people standing in the hallway. I was surprised and touched by everything.

After the eulogy the Preacher said, "would anyone like to say something about Mr. Gutherie, AL." One by one people were standing up and sharing their stories about Dad on how he affected their lives in some way. Right then I realized how respected and admired Dad really was throughout the company, especially with the last five years of the Taurus and Sable program.

We heard the stories about his mentoring, stories about working together, and many stories of friendships. Even Brother Rick got up and spoke about our Dad. When he did my first thought was "here we go again, were in trouble now this will never end," fully knowing how much Rick enjoyed talking in front of an audience. However, that day was totally out of character for him. Amazingly he had only a few loving words to say and he was done. I think even Dad would have been surprised by it. For the first time in his life, Rick did not carry on and on.

I will always remember many heartfelt words that day about Dad, but one in particular will always stand out in my mind. When a co-worker stood up and expressed with such sincerity as he immensely sum up his career saying, "Al was a man who truly gave Ford Motor Company his all." The stories went on for about a half hour they were so moving that all my sad tears turned into happy ones.

Our family truly was touched by it all. We could not have had a better sendoff then that. Their words made us feel prouder and prouder of Dad as they filled our hearts with comfort helping us to overcome our grief.

In the end, Dad's death left a huge gap in our lives. The past three years of our lives were on hold because he needed us. We would not have had it any other way. We learned a lot, we prayed a lot, and **we never gave up or gave in** to this terrible disease called **A.L.S.**

Yes, A.L.S. did take over Dads body. Nevertheless, it did not break his or our spirits. This disease thought it was going to tear the **Gutherie family** apart. I'm proud to say it didn't! We walked away with our heads held high knowing we did everything humanly possible for our loving Dad. As a family, our bond only grew stronger.

We lost our loving Father in January 1988. Nine months later in October of 1988, we lost our beautiful Mother to cancer.

Now, with me being the oldest sibling I felt this strong need to keep our family together. I know mom and Dad were directing me in that way. We were such a close family that I never wanted to see us drift apart.

In the nucleus of a family, the parents in a sense become the wheel of life and the children become the spokes of the wheel. When the wheel falls apart and can no longer hold up the spokes, the spokes drift away. Never did I want my family to go through that. We had been through so much already.

Ever since the Mayo Clinic episode with Dad when we learned this disease could be hereditary, deep down inside I knew there was going to be more tragedies ahead of us. We needed our strength of togetherness to help us get through whatever was lurking in the shadows of our future.

Therefore, I became the wheel so to speak making sure our holiday traditions never died. Every time we were together, you could feel the loving presence of mom and Dad in the room.

For me it was not easy getting over mom and Dad's death. It did take me about 10 years to feel at peace with their loss. Unfortunately, just in time for to me to get stronger to face this fight all over again.

In 1998, this nightmare disease decided to come back and attack the second generation, their children! I could not believe it! We were facing this devastating disease all over again. When will it stop! Enough is enough! It keeps on destroying my family and still to this day 2011; nothing seems to be able to stop it. As if we have not suffered enough here we go again!

CHAPTER 37

Once there were eight, now there are five, Ron, Sue, Rick, their death

Painfully, this demon disease decided it was not through with the **Gutherie family.** In 1998, as the siblings tried to get their lives back on track they found themselves facing this nightmare, this "demon disease" all over again, attacking us.

In my mind, I have this vision of Dad looking down from above with tears running down to earth covering his children with this wall of water, as he tries hard to shield them from this terror. Wishing there was something he could have done to prevent the nightmare we were facing. After all, we as parents have this instinct to protect our children from harm and he was no different. However, how do you fight the impossible odds?

The guilt Dad must have been feeling when he was alive had to be overwhelming, even though it was never his fault, but in a genetic sense, he was responsible. No one has a crystal ball to predict the future. You never know where your roads of life will end up. For us his children, without knowing, had many detours leading nowhere.

Looking back at the day at the Mayo Clinic reliving those haunting words only commences the beginning of our nightmare. **The circle of life and death has begun!**

Brother Ron

The day we found out Ron was starting to have some type of symptoms was unreal. Realizing all hell was going to break out and cause a panic in our family if it turned out to be A.L.S. was too much to bear. I could not think of facing another loved one with this battle. I felt I had to do something to help.

That is when I started searching on the internet, as I used it as a tool to help me find as much information that I could possibly comprehend. I told myself it is about time I became more knowledgeable about this disease.

My searching started to consume me. I started looking at all other neurological diseases that had many similarities to A.L.S., hoping Ron may have had something else. I was in a panic mode thinking if this turns out to be true, now all our lives were at risk too, even our children.

In the beginning, I remember the phone calls Ron made from work to me. Trying to pick my memory about Dad and his disease, hoping the similarities were not the same, as he was making sure he did not frighten his family—yet.

Since I was one of the siblings that were around Dad from the very beginning of his illness, he felt I would be a good source of information for him. I kept trying to reassure Ron that his symptoms sounded completely different from Dad's. Ron counted on me for reassurance, I was his older sister, sadly, all I could do was help with the comparison. I felt helpless.

Still I was trying to understand what the doctors meant when they said this disease is hereditary. Yes, we knew the true meaning of the word, "being passed down through generations." However, the pattern of attack and the age of onset in my eyes should have been the same if the medical field calls this hereditary. I was confused.

First, Ron was 42 with the onset; Dad was 58 when his illness started. Where is the hereditary factor with age? For only that reason, I believed it had to be something else. How were we to know?

We even had Dad's lab report to compare with Ron's. Their blood work did not match up especially the protein levels, which we found out is one of the ways they diagnose this disease. Again, asking the neurologist "shouldn't they have been the same if it's hereditary?" He could not answer my question.

Nevertheless, it did not matter how hard we tried to rule out the comparisons, Ron's diagnosis became the same, **A.L.S.** How sad for him. His youngest daughter was only four years old when they diagnosed him. Sometimes you wonder where's the fairness!

Those haunting words from the Mayo Clinic now became a fact. Unfortunately, we now had **documented proof**; this was an inherited disease, passing down generation-to-generation if no one ever finds a cure. In the end, we **knew**, but we really did not want to **know.**

With mixed emotions as I watched my brother go through what he did only to feel guilty because I was the oldest, thinking this disease attacks in a numerical order. That was very hard to take. Yet, how could I not feel blessed at the same time that it wasn't me.

Yes, with this disease we all have a fifty percent chance of coming down with A.L.S. There was never any scientific proof of what order this disease would take as it attacks the siblings. We were all fighting against the same odds. It's like playing Russian roulette. One by one, the bullet strikes you down. Praying that maybe, just maybe it will pass you by.

Ron lived 8 years with this disease. Seven of them were on a ventilator. He was cared for in his home by his wife and part-time nurses all those years. It certainly was trying for his young wife as she also raised their young family at the same time. Day after day, night after night his children listened to the sound of the machine keeping their Dad alive. I'm sure to them it was reassurance their Dad was still with them.

Seven years is a long time for a family to put their life on hold especially a young mother trying to raise her children by herself. However, she loved Ron and wanted him home with their family. The strong bond they shared along with their faith guided her through.

I have always wondered why Ron wanted to be on a ventilator all those years when he had a choice. I never found the answer to that.

Maybe the family was not ready to let him go. I know you get to that point; we did with Dad.

This I do know for sure, Ron was a very religious man and he left his life in the hands of God, which gave him strength and peace. He knew God would call him home when it was his time. I truly envy that type of mindset at least it makes you face death easier.

Ron and Kim also believed in homeopathic healing as a help for a cure. Maybe he wanted to be a guinea pig, "so-to-speak" and through him, they may find something that would help the future of his children and the rest of the family. Whatever the reason, it was truly a sacrifice. I do not think I would have been as strong.

As the rest of the siblings frantically waited, we never knew when the next bomb was going to drop. Tell me how do you live your life with that threat hanging over you day after day after day!

For me, the more I tried to pretend it did not bother me the more it ate me up inside. In my mind, I felt the only way I could help my siblings was to keep searching on the internet for hope. I could not sit back and do nothing. Maybe, just maybe, in doing so I could find something that could make a difference.

As I took this journey through the internet, I came across a lot of false hope information that only preyed on your vulnerabilities. I can certainly see how it can pull on your heartstrings. I was grateful to have professional guidance along the way to help sort those out. People with frauds like that should be in jail for the rest of their lives to see how it feels when they have no hope left.

I did come across some clinical trials, which always seemed to be hope for the future. Always saying they were a couple years away from FDA approval. Although, looking very promising especially the ones geared toward Familial A.L.S. and the SOD-1 gene, which runs in our family. Sadly, though, with Ron's case, the studies were too new to make a difference for him.

However, now this study knows about our family's history and they promised to keep me informed about advancement. I guess that gives you some hope.

For me, the hardest thing to come to terms with was hearing repeatedly everything was hope for the future. There was **absolutely nothing for now. This disease has been around for years and years would you have thought they were close to finding some hope! How long does research take?**

SISTER SUE

Seven years later in 2005, as if Ron's A.L.S. was not enough agony for our family, my Sister Sue was diagnosed with this demon disease. Ron was still with us although, his body was showing signs the end was near. Not knowing at the time that 2006 was the year, we would lose both of them.

Now there were two family members attacked by A.L.S. I guess we did manage to have a seven year break in between Ron and Sue's onset with this disease. At least that was something.

Again, I was aggressively searching for help for Sue, although this time it was different. With the help of professional experts, bringing to my attention information about an experimental drug study that was showing a lot of promise for A.L.S. was exciting! However, it was only in Phase one which meant there was not enough data on it yet. Sadly, without any luck we found out the study was not successful. Again, I could not just sit and watch her **DIE!**

It was sad to see Sue come down with the disease; she was only 46 years old, the baby of the girls in the family. Again, questioning the hereditary factor of the age of onset, and how it affected Sue's body differently from Dad or Ron's. Still no one could explain that to me. It just didn't make any sense.

Sue lost the use of her arms first. It was pitiful to watch her walk around. Her arms gave you the impression they were tied to her body all the time, as they just hung straight down. Sue was cautious as she walked for fear of falling, as there was no way she could brace herself from a fall. Unfortunately, Sue's lungs were the second muscle to go, way before she even lost the ability to walk. With everything she went through, she never lost her beautiful smile. Proving she was a beautiful person not only on the outside but also inside her heart.

Needless to say, we learned "hereditary" only meant one thing, having the same disease; the way this disease affected our body function first didn't have anything to do with the hereditary factor.

Although, as we did our own tracking with our family's outcome, so far we have learned the age of onset was between 42, and 58. 42 being Ron's age and 58 being Dad's. Also among our family's data, we have learned so far the life expectancy from the beginning of onset to the end, if you choose not to be on a ventilator, was only nine months to a year. That's when we finally came to terms with, no matter where this disease affected the parts of the body first, or whatever the age of onset was, the outcome always ended up the same….**DEATH!**

Throughout Sue's illness, my baby sister made me proud. Not once did I ever hear her complain. She had the inner strength that helped her keep a positive attitude when all hope was gone.

Sue never married nor had children of her own however, she was never alone. She had many true friends and her family around to help her. I guess in a way it was a good thing she never had any children at least the disease ended with her.

Even though she never had children of her own, she shared in all the nieces and nephew's lives. It was important for them to see Aunt Sue come to all their sports activities, which kept her very busy. They all loved her.

I will never forget when she died. It was 2005, a few days past Christmas. Sue wanted to go up north. Not realizing this was going to be her last trip my sister Mary took her. They were very close sisters being one year apart made them almost like twins. The whole time they were gone Sue was having trouble breathing. We thought she might be coming down with a bad cold or even worse pneumonia. Mary took her to the doctor and he put her on antibiotics, which did not help.

When they came home, it was shortly after New Year's 2006. By now, she was having serious problems breathing. My brother-in-law Kurt, Mary's husband took her to the hospital and called me right away, I think it was about three o'clock in the morning when the phone rang, and my heart sank. It all seemed to happen so fast. Since her wishes were never to be on a ventilator, or resuscitated, her lungs collapsed causing her breathing to stop. Sadly, she died in the hospital.

When I got to the hospital, I felt this lonely presence of her being gone as I hurriedly walked down the hallway rushing into her room. I did not want my sister to die alone. She died **seconds** before I got to her room. I believe now she did not want me to see her struggling as she tried to get her last breath. At least she did not die alone. She had my niece and Kurt with her.

When I got to her room, the doctor was still with her. I started crying uncontrollably seeing her lay there not moving. Yet, it was strange; I could still feel her presence in the room as if she wanted to see me one more time before she died. As I bent down over her bed to give her a goodbye kiss, I was alarmed when I felt her body, she still felt warm but all sweaty as if a gush of water came running out of her body. My first thought was maybe she was not dead and she was in a coma. This was my first experience being with someone seconds after their death. The doctor reassured me this was normal, it happens to everyone shortly after death. I could not stop from crying as I hugged her tightly. It was hard for Jim to get me to leave her room. I kept on saying, "I can't believe my baby sister is gone." In a sense, it was like losing a daughter. I do not know what is worse in dealing with a love one's death. If they were sick for awhile and you're somewhat prepared for them to die, or dying suddenly. Whatever, it still a loss as it leaves you with emptiness in your heart! Her death left a big void in everyone's heart.

Although, I was never aware how much her death affected my oldest grandson Josh, who was 13 at the time, until I read the poem he wrote about the first time he heard about her death.

You see for his class project in school he had to compose an essay expressing his feelings about a death of someone close to him. It was ironic how he just experienced Sue's death and how it affected his mind. Never did I realize how much of Sue's death remained bottled up in his heart until he release it on paper.

We as adults always try to keep our emotions under control, especially when our children are around. However, unbeknown to his mom Kimberly, Josh was up in his room the day she received the call Aunt Sue had died. Of course, she just fell apart with the shocking news. Her grief was so horridness that it's no wonder Josh heard the screams of sadness.

I cannot fathom a teenager especially a young boy, expressing his feelings so meaningful; that it brought tears to my eyes when I read it. I knew then there was no better place to keep it embedded in my heart and forever preserved than in my book.

Moments are memories

January 2, 2006

I remember that night very well.
Screaming, yelling, and crying I heard from downstairs.
I thought to myself, what is going on?
I ran down the stairs, with worry on my face.
Then I stopped for a second to see, my mom screaming,
yelling, and crying.
I ran over to her and realized she was gone.
My Aunt Sue had passed.
Going to a new place called heaven.
I think back and remember, all the stories my mom has told me,
about her and Aunt Sue and how they did everything together.
Then I looked at my mom and realized.
This is the worst day of her life.
I sat down by her and I, held her tight and said, "Mom,
everything's going to be alright, "were going to get through this
together.
No more screams were heard,
just the faint sound of sobbing, as my mom spoke back.
"Don't worry my son I'll be alright."
I reached up for her hand, with comfort in sight.
We know that the end was near,
but that does not make it right.

How can someone so young be taken from our sight.
The comfort I speak of, are the moments that was shared,
because, those moments are memories, That will always be spared.

By, Joshua Corey

After Sue's funeral as I sat in the house looking outside. I was grateful it snowing and in the middle of winter. I did not want any of my friends to see how depressed I was. Hoping by spring my heart would have had a chance to mend

I lost my baby sister Sue in January of 2006. In April of the same year, the sounds of Ron's life support silenced. That year was the year from hell. I could not imagine what could possibly happen next to this family.

Unfortunately, we found out!

BROTHER RICK

This time bomb kept on ticking. Now we were starting to see a pattern with this disease. My Brother Rick, who turned 58 in July of 2007, was starting to panic. He knew Dad was 58 when he came down with the disease and was in a panic mode since Ron became ill. I certainly did not blame him. I felt scared as I approached 58 also. Here I am, 63 and still counting my blessing.

All of our minds were playing tricks on us. I actually felt I was having symptoms. I know Rick was feeling the same way although, his feelings were stronger than mine were. At the time, I did not know why regrettably, we all found out. Everyone wonder did he having symptoms for along time and did not want to worry anyone? Was it just his mind playing tricks on him? The only thing we knew for sure was his outcome.

What was scary for us, unfortunately the medical field had no data to back up when the onset would start with any of the siblings, or **even worse, which of us would get this first.**

Therefore, in our frightened minds we tracked our own families' outcome. Convinced ourselves if we were fortunate to get past the age 58, figuring that was how old Dad was when he came down with A.L.S., then this threat of this disease didn't pertain to us anymore. Each year we got closer to that scary age, we held our breath hoping to get older. An age, Rick, Linda, and I had embedded so deeply in our minds no matter how hard we tried; we could never let it go.

Our brother Bob had a completely different attitude about all of this. It never seemed to possess him at least he never let on to us it did.

I cannot begin to tell you how devastated the family was when Rick found out his symptoms were the start of A.L.S. **We were really hoping this disease was through with the Gutherie family.** Hoping someone up above would look down upon our family and feel that we had enough suffering, yet, that never happened!

Not only did Rick have three grown children but he also had two grandkids, now we have the fourth generation having this threat, as the nightmare carries on.

At first, Rick went through a lot of denial and agony trying to come to terms with the disease. He saw what we went through trying to help Sue. At times, it looked like we were only chasing rainbows so he felt it was a waste of his precious time. He did try the homeopathic route with Bob for a while, eventually giving up on that also. Although one good thing came out of that experience with Bob was a renewed stronger brotherly bond between them. They had many funny stories to tell along that journey.

Shortly after that, I think Rick decided to give in and let what will be, be. There was no more fighting the inevitable. Just like the other family members who died before him.

I never saw Rick get depressed. I am sure he had his bad days, but he never showed it around us. Rick knew his only hope was to put his faith in God's hands, just like Ron and Sue; he was at peace with himself. It was amazing to hear him talk; he knew God was going to make him complete again, **MAYBE HE DID!**

The saddest thing for me about losing Rick was our family gatherings. They will never be the same. I will never be able to laugh at his weird sense of humor or listen to his crazy stories. Half the time I was always telling him, "will you please just shut up!"

However mostly, I will miss the nickname he had for me. He was the only one that ever called me Popo. To this day I have no idea how he got PoPo out of Pam. Whenever he would call me on the phone his first words out of his mouth were, "hey PoPo, what do you know." That nickname he had for me will never mean the same it died when he died.

During the last nine months of his life, our bond as siblings became closer. Maybe the reason being we were going through the same mental pain. We always had a close relationship as we were growing up, but now our need for each other was even stronger.

When I started to have problems raising my right arm above my shoulder, my first thoughts were, oh no do I have this! Of course thinking I was having symptoms of ALS. I confided in Rick and he encouraged me to go to MDA clinics where he went. He said if I didn't it would make me sick worrying. All along reassuring me my symptoms were not the same as his.

I hesitated for a couple of weeks because I was scared to find out. The arm just seemed to get worse, I could hardly lift it. Finally, he convinced me to go. I was so grateful he kept pushing me. What they diagnosis was called a frozen shoulder, which probably came from playing too much golf. **If there's such a thing as playing too much.** I was so relieved. For now I could take a deep breathe and continue to play golf.

Rick was always encouraging me in many different ways throughout my life. I remember at Sue's funeral, I wrote a little story about her and I playing golf together in my Ladies Invitational, which having the same interest made our bond closer. Rick felt it was such a touching story that a couple days later he called and said, "you know what Popo, Chicken Soup For the Women's Golfer Soul is looking for short stories for their next issue." I said, "okay, what does that mean to me?" He said, "you need to submit the story about you and Sue, the one you read at her funeral." All I could say was "yeah right!"

Well, thanks to Rick I did. To my surprise, they published it. Because of that, he gave me the confidence to do something I always wanted to do. Write a book about our family's fight with this terrible disease; unfortunately a never-ending story.

It was 2007, Rick was in a wheelchair now, and he could no longer move his legs, could not dress himself, and because he could no longer move his arms needed help eating and with his personal care. Now his breathing was in stress and he knew it was only a matter of time for him. Like Sue, he did not want to be on a ventilator. He decided to admit himself into a nursing home. It was getting very difficult for his wife Karen to take care of him at home. He witnessed what mom went through with Dad's care and he never wanted his wife to go through that with him.

A week before Christmas I was hosting the family Christmas party at my house. My brother was not one to miss any family gathering. He loved being around the family. Even more so, he enjoyed being the center of attention. This year was no different; he was looking forward to coming. I had a terrible feeling the day before my party, as I told Jim I felt this strong need to go to the nursing home to visit with Rick. When we got there, he looked great. He was cracking jokes with the staff making me feel like I was worrying for nothing, even though I was feeling uncomfortable with the way he was breathing.

When Rick talked it looked like it was hard for him to catch his breath in-between his words. I could see his chest go up and down as if he was running out of air. However, not once did it look like he was in a stressed situation with his lungs. When we left, I gave him a big kiss and told him I loved him and reminded him about the family Christmas party the following day. His response was, "are you kidding, I'm not going to miss that. Angie and Karen are coming up to get me in the morning to bring me there."

To this day, we do not know what happened to Rick in the middle of the night. The morning staff found him outside his bed hanging on with one arm to the rail of bed as if he was trying to get in a kneeling position. Of course, they said no one heard his commotion in the middle of the night. I know it had to have been loud because Rick was a tall man.

Now, here was a man that could not move his legs, and the only strength he had left was in one arm. How could he have gotten out of bed? He could not even roll over, or reach his cell phone that was on his table to call Karen and Angie. Who knows, maybe in his last moments he found the will to do just that, we will never know.

When the staff found Rick in that position they got him back in bed and called Karen and Angie immediately. They advised them to hurry to the nursing home because Rick's breathing was very erratic and shallow; it was only a matter of time. It was about one o'clock in the afternoon when Angie called my daughter Kristie, as she was already at the Christmas gathering. They have always been close cousins. When Angie said, "I don't want to alarm everyone but Dad isn't doing well at all." Immediately Kristie and Jim got in the car and went to the nursing home to be with them. I knew something was wrong although I was trying to believe my brother was still coming and they just needed more help getting him into the car. Sadly, he passed away shortly before Kristie and Jim got there. Thank God, his wife, daughter, was with him.

I was in the middle of preparing dinner when I got the phone call. I have no idea how the rest of the dinner got finished. All I remember was Jim saying, "honey, he's gone." I could not believe it we just saw him the day before and he looked great he was in such a good mood. That was my Brother Rick always happy. If my last vision of my brother was sad ones it would have been hard to bear, a memory I did not want for the rest of my life. Thank goodness, I was able to tell him I loved him one more time before we had to say goodbye.

That day the family Christmas party was so quiet you did not even hear the younger grandkids playing. My heart sank with sadness thinking about Rick's beautiful little grandkids. They were never going to see him again. I could not help putting myself in that scenario. No one felt like saying anything, only tears shed.

In my heart, I knew Rick did not miss our family Christmas party that day, I could feel his presence in the room. Somehow, someway I knew he would find a way to be there.

Rick passed away in 2007, one year after Sue. There is no doubt he certainly did it with a statement. Just the way he did everything, so no one would ever forget. **THAT WAS OUR RICK!**

CHAPTER 38
Being tested for the SOD-1 Gene

As I sit here finishing my book finding it hard to still digest everything that has happened in my family trying my best to come to terms with it all makes me realize only one thing, enough is enough! I am tired of writing about this destruction. Seeing my siblings slowly demolished. **One by one, this disease is bringing them down!**

I'm definitely tired of seeing the worried look of fear on my daughter's faces. Although, they admitted to me they never dwell on the what-ifs, but how could they not have if it's in the back of their minds. Even though I was scared to death for the future of the whole Gutherie family, naturally I was mainly scared for my kids and grandkids. I had to find a way to do something. I wanted this threat lifted off their shoulders. No way did I want them to go through their life in fear of when and if this disease will strike. **However, what were my options!**

Then I remembered back in 2008, I was receiving update information on a study at a University Hospital in Georgia. This study was focusing on Familial A.L.S. and the SOD-1 gene my family carries. I figured now was the time for me to contact them to see what I could do.

By taking a DNA test, this study was giving me the opportunity to find out if I was a carrier of this gene. My reason behind that was, hopefully to relieve the burden of this threat from my children. Figuring if the test came back positive and I had the gene, I could volunteer to be a candidate for research. Who knows, maybe I could be the one to help find the answer, of course hoping all along I did not carry the gene. Trying to protect my children was the only way I could get my nerve up to follow through with this.

It certainly was not an easy decision for me. The reality was when the test came back I would soon know if I was facing a life or death scenario. Knowing for sure what lies ahead of you with your life was a frightening thought.

In my eyes, I had to go ahead with this, having this disease on my mind since Ron's death was a lot of mental anguish. I did not want my children going through years of fear like me. For my sake and my children's, I had to know one way or another. I did not want to wait until the bomb went off for me.

It was July 2009, I sent away for the DNA test. I told the girls I was doing it hoping as summer got busy they would forgot all about it. If it were not for the support from Jim backing me up all the way with my decision, I probably would not have gone through with it. I have to say mentally I was not here that whole summer.

In September of 2009, on the 19th, as you may wonder why that exact date stays in my mind, amazingly it was **my birthday**. That afternoon the kids were all coming over to our house to help celebrate my birthday. I will always remember when the phone rang that afternoon. Jim was out cutting the lawn. I quickly noticed on the caller ID that it was the University calling me, my heart sank. I don't even know if I was breathing, so many frightening thoughts were running through my mind. I hesitantly picked up the phone; it was the hospital on the other end letting me know they had my test results back. They were being very cautious with me making sure I still wanted to know my results over the phone. That's when I became frightening and almost lost it.

You see, in the very beginning before they even agreed to do the test I had to sign a waiver letting them know how I wanted to know about my test results, on the phone, or in person. If I chose in person, they would arrange for me to come to Georgia. In addition to that, they would make sure a specialist in psychiatry was in the room with me when they gave me the news. They were all about protecting your mental state. I reassured them I was not changing my mind, and yes I wanted to know over the phone, I really did not want to wait any longer. I could not believe I was saying that, all of a sudden, I was not scared anymore. Still they were being cautious with me asking if someone was in the room with me before they gave me my information. When I heard that I thought, this does not sound good maybe I should go out and get Jim. **My heart sank and** I froze on the phone holding my breath. I felt my heart beating so fast I thought I was going to pass out. It seemed like hours before I answered them back, but in reality, it was only seconds. I finally told them no one was in the room with me but reassured them if I needed someone, my husband Jim was out in the back yard cutting the lawn. I was shocked at myself that I even said that, still holding my breath.

Then I heard the words that gave me my life, my children lives, and my precious grandkids life back. **"YOU'RE NOT CARRYING THIS GENE!"** I thought I was dreaming. All I could say was, "I'm sorry could you please say that again." I heard this voice on the other end say, "you don't have a chance of getting A.L.S., you're not a carrier of this gene."

I could not believe what I just heard how could that be. I know each sibling has a fifty percent chance of carrying this gene, how was I spared? This was the first time in my life I became a **HUGH** winner.

I told the person on the phone that today was my birthday and she just gave me the best present ever, and in turn, I couldn't wait to give my present to my children. **"Our lives back!"**

After I hung up the phone, I was crying so hard I could hardly see. I ran outside to Jim and leaped into his arms knocking him down. He did not know what hit him. He kept saying, "honey what's wrong, are you alright?" I was in such a state of shock; I could not say anything. I just kept on crying and shaking all over.

Finally, I settled down enough to say I got the phone call and **"I don't have it."** I did not have to say anything else, he knew. We both started crying holding each other tightly with the sound of the lawn mower still roaring in the background. I think if my neighbors saw us that day they would have called the police thinking something was seriously wrong with us.

I was so overwhelmed, that I had a hard time not sharing this news right away with my girls. Even though I was climbing the walls with excitement, I wanted to wait until my party to tell them. I needed to see the looks of my girls' faces when I gave them this wonderful gift. To tell you the truth, even though it was in the middle of the afternoon, Jim and I couldn't wait to have a drink so we could be calm before the kids got here.

When it came time for dinner as usual, both families arrived at the same time. All the grandkids were running in the house trying to beat each other to say happy birthday to me first. At that moment, I lost it. I could no longer hold back my tears especially when I saw everyone walking in the door. As I stood there crying uncontrollably right away my two daughters sensed something was wrong with me. It was obvious to Jim I was going to have a hard time getting my composure to tell the kids my news. He just hugged me tightly to calm me down and said, "kids everyone settle down, mom has something to say."

Kristie right away with a panic in her voice said "mom did you get your test results back, tell me, did you!" Well that did not help my situation I started crying even more. "Mom," she said again with fear in her voice. "Tell us, did you?" When I settled down a bit I said, "today is my birthday but I'm giving you kids a present instead the best present ever, I'm not carrying the A.L.S. gene."

Josh, who is the oldest grandchild 14 at that time said, "does that mean you're not going to get that disease Nana?" When he said that I could not believe he even gave it a second thought. As a teenager, they do not seem to pay too much attention to things like that their having too much fun.

I felt bad thinking he must have been worried about this ever since Sue's death, as he derived a conclusion on his own figuring out the heredity factor. This was something I did not want the grandkids to know until they were old enough to understand. I really did not think he put too much thought into how many generations this disease would affect our family, only thinking about his Nana, me coming down with this. I was so glad I was able to take away that fear. It made me cry even more to know how much he **loved** me. Of course, all that did was start all of us crying all over again as we gathered around with a group hug. It was the best birthday present ever!

It took me awhile before I told my brothers and sisters. I did not know how to approach them. Here I was out of the woods and they still had that threat. In my eyes, it was just as selfish as waving a piece of candy in their faces and not sharing it. I just wished I could have found a way to give them that gift also.

When my sister-in- law Karen found out about my good news, the first thing she said to me was, "Pam I think God has a plan for you, that's why he has spared you." Can you imagine her saying that to me after loosing her husband? I told her while trying to hold back my tears, "I would love for him to give me a sign so I could get started on the plan right away". Then she said, "well maybe he has with your story about our family, did you ever think of that? Who knows maybe it will help bring more awareness to this disease. Opening up more avenues to generate more funds for A.L.S. research in hopes to find a cure, then that will truly be a gift from God, and you can feel proud that you contributed." After she said that, I started to choke up again and could not talk. "Pam" she said "are you okay?" I told her "I have always hoped for that to happen. I know I will never give up until there is a cure.

CHAPTER 39
Will this ever stop, sister Linda

After seeing what I went through with my DNA test for the mutated SOD-1 gene, Linda decided she was going to have it done also. Not wanting anyone to know she was going through with this except her husband Terry, was a stressful decision for her to make. Yet she felt the same way I did, she needed to do it for her children's sake. Even knowing there was a fifty percent chance it could be positive it was a risk she wanted to take.

When her test came back, Linda was scared to find out the results. Having second thoughts, it played on her mind for three months before she finally got her nerve up to take the phone call. Still at this point just she and Terry knew.

Never did I want to put in my book my Sister Linda's devastating news. I was hoping for some good news to write about but that never happened.

It was November of 2009, when Linda finally took the phone call from the clinic. There she was my courageous sister, finding out she had the mutated SOD-1 gene that runs in our family. To this day scientists cannot find any data in your DNA that tells you when this disease will start its attack, all they know for sure is you are a carrier of A.L.S.

Nevertheless, she was still sitting on a time bomb mentally hearing the ticking everyday. Only this time her mental anguish was worse than before. She just went from one nightmare to catastrophe! No one warned us about this scenario.

With Linda turning 58 in September 2010, only reinforced our beliefs about that scary age of 58 that kept on haunting most of us. Now it was her turn, what a **horrendous** weight to be playing on her mind.

After that phone call, the study wanted her to fly to Georgia where this study took place. Since she was able to have someone go with her, she took Terry her husband. They performed many neurological tests to see if there were any signs of the disease starting yet. To her relief there was nothing, although, it still did not take away her fear that now she was a candidate. Unfortunately, she still couldn't be part of any study until the onset of this disease started, which was one of the main reason we both took this test. No one informed us about that. Therefore, your life still ends up in a state of limbo.

I remember the Christmas of 2010. I was hosting the family Christmas party. Everyone was having such a good time; I know Linda did not want to spoil the moment to tell me about her fear that maybe this might be her last Christmas.

Not once did Linda say anything to me about finding out the results of her SOD-1 gene test. I of all people her big sister and her best friend. I could have reassured her and told her it still did not mean she would come down with the disease. Nevertheless, I know it would not have made a difference she was smarter than that.

Linda and I have always shared the love between sisters. However, our bond never started to grow until the year she was graduating from high school. That is when we became best friends. Since there is five years difference in our ages, when you are younger that's a lot. In fact, Linda was only 13 years old when I got married.

Our friendship grew more when Jim and I returned to the states from his military duty. That year for some reason, Linda needed her big sister even more. I never knew why but I was grateful she wanted my attention.

When Jim I and our daughter Kimberly moved into the city, which was many miles away from my parents' home, it was a hard adjustment for Linda to make, especially with us just getting back from being away for two years. At the time, it was the first job Jim had so we couldn't be too picky.

Everyday when Linda was done with school she would drive into the city to keep Kimberly and I company while Jim was working. I really think being a first time aunt enticed her a little bit more. Ever since then our friendship and love grew.

Over the years, we have shared many happy times and cried together with the sad times. Terry, her husband, always got a big kick out of the way Linda and I would always carry on with a conversation. One of us would always start it and the other knew how to finish it. Never did we have to fill in the middle; we always knew what the other was going to say. Meanwhile, always leaving our husbands in the dark wondering what in the world did we just say? I always thought that type of connection was strange, which is something you only expect from twins.

If I ever needed someone to lean on besides Jim, she was there. It went both ways. That is why her need for me now is greater then ever.

In March of 2010, my sister and best friend felt she was having symptoms of A.L.S. Again, without telling anyone she and Terry flew back to the University Hospital for more testing. She was hoping it was her mind playing tricks again; after all, she was just there in November. The pressure of her not knowing if this was really happening was making her sick inside. She was tired of going back and forth and not finding anything. Again putting her through many tests, only this time they found out **A.L.S. had started its attack!** Within four months, this demon disease started its destruction on my sister.

Here it is July 2010, and even though she has lost the ability to move her left arm she is still with us and fighting as hard as she can. Its amazing how her family has pulled together to fight this disease with her. It reminds me of Linda fighting all over again for Dad. Only this time there's more hope on the horizon.

Linda knew about a newer study that was available. She always kept it in the back of her mind if she decided to take that route.

However, it took a couple of months before they gave her the go-ahead by then she was a lot weaker.

One of the criteria to enter this study was good lung capacity, which is always a great concern with this disease. What was interesting to our family's situation this study has been working on a new chemical approach geared to attack this gene, which Familial A.L.S. families carry. It is the hope of these scientists that it will stop the gene from mutating. Whether this mutation is the cause of activating this disease is unknown.

In October of 2010, she entered this study. This procedure in the way they administer this drug was very intense and invasive. Nevertheless, Linda was determined to go through with this no matter how bad it hurt. She felt very positive this was the answer to our prayers.

Unfortunately, just like any other study there was one drawback, it was a **placebo** study, meaning you have no idea if you were getting the real drug. That we didn't understand when we signed this waiver the clinic sent to us in the beginning.

I have a hard time understanding why the FDA demands this of studies especially where people are going to die anyway. These patients have nothing to lose and everything to gain. They must know all they're doing is playing Russian roulette with these patients' lives. This is their last hope. After all everyone signs a waiver before you begin this study, so why not let it be their choice, they are the ones that are **DYING!** Therefore, we sit and wait hoping she didn't go through all of this for nothing.

Thanksgiving was just around the corner, and Linda gave thanks with her beautiful family that she was still here. At this stage in her illness, she was starting to feel the effects of her other arm **becoming weaker.** In addition, she was scared to death about her breathing It was now compromised.

Her biggest fear with this disease was it would have the same effect on her as it did with Sue. How in the world did Sue manage to get by without the use of both arms? She remained that way for months before her lungs collapsed causing her death. Day after day having someone feed her, bathe her, and even clean up after she used the bathroom. These were all unimaginable thoughts; one Linda knew was coming, unless she found a miracle.

I don't know how strong I can be anymore. Within four months, this horrific disease has attacked another member of my family, my best friend, my loving sister. I could not believe it when she finally confided in me. I was upset at her for not sharing with me in the beginning and sad at the same time because we both knew **she was in for the biggest fight of her life.**

Throughout these tragedies with losing my Dad, my mom, my two brothers' and sister, it has been very difficult for me to handle. Yet, my hands are tied; there is nothing I can do. It is impossible to turn back the clock and impossible to fight the odds. **Nevertheless, I will never give-up, or give-in.** Only this time I am scared that I **will** fall apart with Linda's demise.

I remember one time when we were both crying together over the loss of Sue as we stood there hugging each other. Linda said" I don't know what I would do if I lost you." Jokingly just to break up the tension I said "don't worry I'm not going anywhere." We both just stood there in silence thinking we will never know when it would be our turn. It's those times when reality hits you right in the face. Who would have guessed this was in her future too.

My sister Linda has always been a very strong person. If there is a way to find hope, it will happen to her. Everything she did for Dad when he was ill will come back to her two fold. We know Dad is up above watching her, protecting her, holding her hand, trying to do his best to guide her through this journey. I know his heart is breaking because there is nothing he can do. Only be her guardian angel. For now, all we can do is *pray*, and maybe, just maybe Linda will find her **MIRACLE.**

I guess in the end, if a person was believer of a higher entity, then it can give you a feeling of peace knowing your loved one did find their miracle.

Linda did spend one more Christmas with us, 2010. Only this year I didn't want to have the family Christmas party. I was afraid Linda wouldn't make it. Thank goodness, Jim and the girls talked me into it; at least I was able to have one more Christmas with her.

Regrettably, my sister Linda lost her battle with A.L.S. Never did I want to end my story about her in this way. In my heart, I truly thought we finally had this disease beat.

It was Wednesday, February 9, 2011. I was going over to Linda's house to help Terry with her. At this point in Linda's illness, she was still able to walk, however she did lose the ability to move her arms. Just like Sue. She had a minute movement in one hand, but that also was rapidly going. She was using a by-pass machine to help her breathe at night. It wasn't like a ventilator that did the breathing for you. However, I know she was at the point of needed one, which the family was struggling with that decision. Her appetite was gone, and she could barely talk. Yet, she still looked good to us.

Yes, all the signs were there but we weren't looking for them. After the couple of trial studies she went through, along with the help of "medical M." she used," we were still hoping something would work. At least it bought her more time for she lived the longest in our family with this disease.

I know the whole family was in shock because it seemed within four days she went from looking good to dying. Unfortunately, that Wednesday will stay imbedded in my memory forever.

I was always fearful of being in the room when another loved one of mine died. I went through that with my mom, and still to this day, 22 years later, it still haunts me. Although, that morning when I walked into Linda's house around 11:00 am and noticed she was still in bed sleeping my heart stopped because **I KNEW.**

Her husband Terry saw my concerned look on my face and reassured me everything was all right, justifying her sleeping in this late of a restless night, so he was letting her get caught up. For a moment, I thought well he knows best and I decided to relax a little. As we sat in the kitchen having coffee talking and sharing tears for our Linda, it was around 12:00 when Terry said, "well I have to wake her up now she needs her medication, and they need to be so many hours apart."

When we both went into the room and I saw her just laying there, I was holding my breath with fear. Terry gently shook her saying "wake upLinda, its time to take your medication." Alarmingly she was not responding until he said, "Pam is here." then she picked her head up as if she wanted to see me.

As we struggled to get her in a sitting position on the side of the bed, she astounded me when I saw her face. Her eyes were sunken and her face was all puffy. I couldn't get over her eyes, they were so strange as if she was looking right through me in bewilderment. I then realized her eyes were dilated to the point you could not even see her pupil. I started shaking, yet I did not want to show my fears to Terry. He was so concerned about making sure she had her medication. It was all he could do to focus on.

I sat on the edge of the bed holding her hand and noticed they were all blotchy and red, as if she was freezing cold, but it was the opposite, she was all sweaty. She kept on trying to tell me something as I tried to put my ear close to listen. Her lips were moving but I never heard a word. When I said what, she looked right at me with a smile on her face and repeated it. Still I could not hear anything, so I smiled back and pretended that I knew what she was trying to tell me.

Maybe someday her words will come to me, although I have no doubt they were loving words, because of our special bond between sisters.

After Terry gave her the pills, all she wanted to do was go back to sleep. We laid her down gently; while I was trying to get her feet up on the bed and organized, I noticed they were all blotchy with redness too. I knew then it was only a matter of time. Her beautiful body was shutting down.

Still not wanting to panic Terry I immediately called his son Terry Allen and told him of my fears. As I was talking on the phone a nurse came to the door, I was so relieved she was there, for I felt myself choking with fear, fear of not wanting to be here when Linda died. However, I could not leave Terry alone. As soon as I knew Terry was fine with the nurse there, I almost ran out the door. I could not wait to get out of the house. I knew Terry Allen would be there soon, and that was a good thing. His wife Nadia and their children were closely behind.

Addy, her youngest son was just coming home from high school, and unfortunately, her middle son Ryan was flying home from Germany, sadly he did not get there in time. I was feeling sad knowing what they were all going to witness although in my heart, I knew it was meant to be. There is no doubt in my mind that all our loved ones that had gone before her were also with her, especially our **DAD.** I have to say he must have put in a good word with above because her exit was peaceful.

Jim and I were having dinner when the phone rang; as he answered, his voice became somber. He did not have to say a thing; I knew my sister was gone. I could not stop from crying, I know it was building up in me for a long time. Life without my best friend, my loving sister will be hard to face. Nevertheless, when I close my eyes at night I know she is there. This disease has to stop taking my family. I will never feel at peace with myself until I know everyone is safe and healthy.

EPILOGUE

With my story ending, I find this amazing coincidence between my Dad and me. How we both could relate to Atlanta Georgia when this disease first came into our lives. Only to be happening 22 years apart, as if it was meant to revolve in a full circle as it affected our lives differently.

In 1985, my Dad was going down to **Atlanta Georgia,** where the Taurus and Sable plant was located making sure they were ready for their big launch. It was his job as Chief Engineer to see them from the design floor all the way through production.

It was in the airport going to Georgia where he took his fall because he lost his balance and his legs just gave out from under him. Unbeknown to him it was when his fear of this disease started.

Also in Atlanta, Georgia, my fear ended. This is where the University Hospital is located that tested my DNA for the mutated SOD-1 gene that runs in our family. Fortunately, for me it turned out to be good news, I was not carrying this gene.

For my Dad, unfortunately his trip to Georgia is where the terrible incident of this attack started that ended his life. For me**, Georgia is where they tested my DNA**, that I thank God every day it was the best news ever, it gave me back my life. **Was this destiny for both of us?**

With this debilitating disease, there are so many lives at stake, especially in my family. We need to find hope and we need to silence this destruction, and we need to pray, **because we cannot do it alone! Mostly I need my family in heaven to know that I will never stop trying to find ways to bring attention to this horrendous disease until the day someone finds a cure!**

About the Author:
Pamela M. (Gutherie) Woods

Pamela was born and raised in Michigan, graduated from Walled Lake Central High School in 1965. The following year married her husband Jim. They have two beautiful daughters Kimberly, and Kristina, and five grandchildren; Joshua 16, Nicholas 13, Nolan 10, Nathan 9, and Sarah 6. She has an undying love for the game of golf and watching her grandchildren participate in their sports, filling retirement life to the fullest. Writing experience was a short story written for the Chicken Soup Book Series "For the Women's Golfer Soul." Title; "If there is Golf in heaven I know my Sister Sue is playing."

Resources:

- Automotive Information: October 1985 issue of SAS magazine

- Medical information provided from Mayo Clinic Department of Neurology1985,Addison L. Gutherie- medical records

- High School years genealogy provided by: Thomas A. Gutherie—Cousin

- Communication information provided from Addison L. Gutherie—medical records—The Med-Com Company, Columbus, Ohio 1985

- Photography: provided by daughter, Kimberly Corey

- Poem: by grandson, Joshua Michael Corey

CPSIA information can be obtained at www.ICGtesting.com
Printed in the USA
BVOW031736071011

273020BV00001B/1/P